Tactical Chess Exchanges

Gennady Nesis

Collier Books
Macmillan Publishing Company
New York

Maxwell Macmillan Canada
Toronto

Collier Books
Macmillan Publishing Company
866 Third Avenue, New York, NY   10022

Maxwell Macmillan Canada, Inc.
1200 Eglinton Avenue East
Suite 200
Don Mills, Ontario M3C 3N1

Macmillan Publishing Company is part of the Maxwell Communication Group of Companies

Library of Congress Cataloging-in-Publication Data

Nesis, G. E. (Gennadiĭ Efimovich)
    Tactical chess exchanges / Gennady Nesis—1st Collier Books ed.
        p.   cm.
    ISBN 0–02–029437–9
    1. Chess—Middle games.   I. Title.
GV1450.3.N48   1991   91–3588
794.1′23—dc20   CIP

Macmillan books are available at special discounts for bulk purchases for sales promotions, premiums, fund-raising, or educational use. For details, contact:

Special Sales Director
Macmillan Publishing Company
866 Third Avenue
New York, NY   10022

First Collier Books Edition 1991
10 9 8 7 6 5 4 3 2 1
Printed in Great Britain

Contents

Foreword

At the end of the sixties, Yuri Balashov, in those days a young master destined to become a famous Grandmaster, chess instructor and Anatoly Karpov's second, was captivated by the creative genius of Robert Fischer.

Neither could we, his friends, remain indifferent, and I shall always remember his reply to one of my questions regarding the now legendary player. He said: "Do you realize, Fischer almost never has any *bad* pieces. He exchanges them, and the bad pieces remain with his opponents".

Well, no doubt we all wish to sacrifice effectively, but we attach less importance to *exchanging* effectively. But believe an experienced chess-player and instructor – only a good bishop can be sacrificed, a bad bishop can only be lost. So read this book carefully, reflect on it and learn how to exchange!

Grandmaster Yuri Razuvayev

1   Linking all stages of the game

What is the essence of chess? Is there a simple answer to this question? Here is what ex-World Champion Botvinnik wrote concerning this question, in his book *An Algorithm of Chess*:

"In my opinion, the process of chess is based essentially on interlinking exchanges. The objective of these interlinking exchanges is a relative gain . . . . . of material or of positional value. There are no other and cannot be any other objectives. At the end of the game these exchanges must lead to a gain of infinitely large magnitude (to mate)".

Botvinnik's work was devoted to developing chess-computer programs. For a scientific worker the concept of the exchange has a wide and abstract meaning. However, the more literal concrete meaning of exchange—the alternate elimination of pieces—plays a vital role in chess. In fact, the exchange is the fundamental method of transposing play from the middlegame into the endgame. Furthermore, the simplification resulting from the exchange is an essential method of realizing an advantage. The process of chess being dynamic, all

the basic stages of the game are interrelated—the opening, the middlegame and the endgame.

The dynamics of chess consists of a gradual change in the situation on the chessboard, even after an apparently unimportant series of moves. In addition to gradual changes, it is usually possible to isolate critical moments in which there are abrupt, qualitative transformations.

These are the critical points at which the game transposes from one phase into another. Their study is one of the most complex problems of modern chess theory.

Naturally, the arrangement of the pieces in the opening will have a decisive influence on the plans of the players in the middlegame.

The link between the opening and the strategy adopted by the players in the middlegame can be well illustrated by various opening gambits. In a whole series of gambit systems, where the sacrifice of material has a realistic, unpretentious character, this link can often be traced right through the game, from opening to endgame. The player accepting the "Greek gift" is forced into defensive play for a long time, whereas his opponent, with the pawn deficit, must energetically and persistently take the initiative. The following game serves to illustrate this.

Kristiansson–Roberts
World Student Team
Championship 1967

The Morra Gambit

1	e4	c5
2	d4	cxd4
3	c3	dxc3
4	♘xc3	♘c6
5	♘f3	d6
6	♗c4	♘f6

After only six moves the plans of both sides are already apparent. The Morra Gambit has been played, known among Austrian chessplayers since the end of the nineteenth century. The idea of the gambit is simple: White acquires an advantage in development and space for the loss of a pawn. Is this sufficient compensation for the material loss?

Black has no weaknesses for the time being, but he has to think

about his development and castling. After the natural 7 0-0 e6, White brings his forces into a state of 'battle readiness' by some scheme such as ♗f4, ♕e2, ♖fd1, ♖ac1, to create the possibility of concrete attacking play against any sort of set-up chosen by his opponent. However, Black can set up a well-defended position. The Gambit variation encourages White to embark on energetic operations.

7 e5!?

This move, resulting in fierce middlegame complications, was undoubtedly selected as a strategical and psychological complement to the sharp opening.

7 ... dxe5

Naturally, not 7 ... ♘xe5?, since after 8 ♘xe5 dxe5 9 ♗xf7+ Black loses his queen.

In Veiraush–Mail, 1957, after 7 ... ♘g4 play did not reach the endgame: 8 e6! (*8 ... fxe6 9 ♘g5*) 9 ♗f4 g6 10 ♘d4 ♘ge5 11 ♗xe5 dxe5 (*11 ... fxe5 12 ♘xc6*) 12 ♘xc6 ♕xd1+ 13 ♖xd1 bxc6 14 ♘b5! 1–0.

8 ♕xd8+ ♘xd8

Let us pause for a moment.

The queens have been exchanged, but has play transposed into an endgame? The endgame is sharply distinguished from the other two stages of play by the active participation of the kings in the battle. An exception to this definition is a complex endgame with the heavy pieces still present, in which the king can still be the object of an immediate attack. "In the endgame the king is an active piece"—this aphorism is not simply a play on words. As shown in practice, the strength of a centralized king is approximately equal to that of a minor piece. Is such an evaluation valid in the situation which has arisen in the present game? Not yet. To confirm this conclusion, we make use of Matulovic–Vincenti, 1954, which continued: 8 ... ♔xd8?! 9 ♘g5! ♔c7? (9 ... ♘a5! is better: 10 ♘xf7+ ♔e8 11 ♘xe5 ♘xc4, though here again White has the advantage) 10 ♘xf7 ♖g8 11 ♘b5+ ♔b8 12 ♘xe5! ♘xe5 13 ♗f4 (2) ♘fd7 14 ♗xg8 a6 15 ♘d4 ♔a7 16 0-0! 1–0.

So, in spite of the absence of queens, play is clearly still in the middlegame, in which the precarious position of the black king may prove decisive to the outcome of the game.

9	♘b5	♖b8
10	♘xe5	e6
11	♘c7+	

After 11 ♘xa7 material equality would be restored, but the black king would then succeed in escaping to a safe place and the chances for the two sides would be equalized. But is this the spirit of this romantic gambit? No, White continues his attack.

11	...	♔e7
12	♗e3	

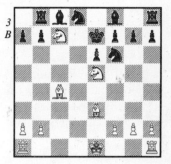

with the unambiguous threat of 13 ♗c5 Mate!

12	...	♘c6

An interesting complication would arise after the king fork— 12 ... ♔d6. It would not be simple for White to punish the impudent king. For instance: 13 ♗f4 ♔xc7! (13 ... ♘h5 is bad, hoping for 14 ♘xf7++? ♔e7 15 ♗g5+ ♔xf7 16 ♗xd8 ♗b4+, in view of 14 ♘b5+!) 14 ♘xf7+ ♔b6 15 ♘xd8 (comparatively better is 15 ♘xh8!) 15 ... ♗b4+ 16 ♔f1 ♖xd8 17 ♗xb8 ♘e4 and, disregarding his material deficit, Black takes the initiative. Or 13 0-0-0+ ♔xc7 14 ♖xd8 ♔xd8 15 ♘xf7+ (15 ♖d1+ ♘d5) 15 ... ♔e8 16 ♘xh8 and the white knight is doomed. In these variations the activity of the king looks justified—all because of the absence of queens. However, the correctness of such a strategy depends on an evaluation of the main continuation 13 ♘b5+ ♔xe5 14 ♗d4+ when the centralized black king would fall under fire from the whole white army.

13 0-0-0

Renewing the threat 14 ♗c5 Mate.

13	...	♘d7
14	♘xf7!	♔xf7
15	♗xe6+	

A small combination, clearly with middlegame motives—poor development of the black pieces and the precarious position of the king.

| 15 | ... | ♔g6 |

On 15 ... ♔e7 either 16 ♗xd7 ♗xd7 17 ♗c5+, or the more effective 16 ♖he1! is good for White.

| 16 | ♗xd7 | ♗xd7 |
| 17 | ♖xd7 | |

At last a clear endgame position has emerged, but in the transition from the middlegame to the endgame White has not merely recaptured the pawn sacrificed on his third move, he has captured another pawn. It should be pointed out that this transition was accomplished tactically.

17	...	♘e5
18	♖d5	♖c8
19	♖xe5	♖xc7+
20	♔b1	a6
21	♖hd1	♔f7
22	♗b6	♖e7
23	♖f5+	♔e6

White now has an opportunity of exploiting the unsatisfactory

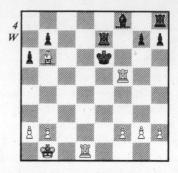

disposition of the black pieces, forcing a final transition of play from a complex endgame into a won pawn ending. A good example of the concept of simplifying with the object of realizing a material advantage.

24	♖xf8	♖xf8
25	♖e1+	♔d7
26	♖xe7+	♔xe7
27	♗c5+	♔e8
28	♗xf8	♔xf8
29	♔c2	

Black resigned.

We should mention that gambit variations are employed not just in the old romantic openings, at times they are used in popular opening systems, where material sacrifice is associated with the objective of seizing the initiative. The competitive battles in modern chess demand that competitors should possess and arsenal of sharp developing systems. In the last few years, young chess-players' average standard of play has increased significantly. Owing to the enormous number of chess periodicals, information becomes available within a short space of time even in the remotest corners of the world. There are many tournaments run on the Swiss system, in which competitors with the same number of points play each other in every round. Such tournaments are reminiscent of an exciting sports race. To win such a tournament, it is imperative that the competitor possess a variety of sharp opening systems even when playing with the black pieces. Whereas in a match or in a round-robin competition, with players of roughly equal strength, one of the leaders, playing with black pieces, can afford to weaken and settle for a draw, in a tournament run on the Swiss system such a draw could cost the peaceful leader his place and, with a large number of competitors, result in a throng of players catching him up.

We now examine a game from the European Youth Championship, in which the Leningrad master Khalifman, playing the King's Indian Defence against the popular Sämisch system, chooses a variation in which a pawn is sacrificed, and transposes into a complex endgame. Black is compensated for his material loss by a strong, persistent initiative.

Arlandi–Khalifman
European Junior Championship, Groningen, 1985/86

King's Indian Defence

1	d4	♘f6
2	c4	g6

3	♘c3	♗g7
4	e4	d6
5	f3	0-0
6	♗e3	c5!?

This interesting method of playing against the Sämisch system has again gained popularity in recent times. Its advantage is that White is forced to show his intentions immediately. 7 d5 leads to the Benoni system, for instance, 7 ... e6 8 ♘ge2 exd5 9 cxd5 h5! This original idea of the Latvian players gives Black a satisfactory game.

7 dxc5

The main line, White accepts the sacrifice, but Black acquires control of the open d-file.

7	...	dxc5
8	♕xd8	♖xd8
9	♗xc5	♘c6
10	♖d1	

A new idea.

Despite the exchange of queens, the struggle bears a middlegame character. Until quite recently it was considered that White can gain the advantage with 10 ♘d5 ♘d7 11 ♗a3 (an interesting draw was reached in a game between

Salov and Glek, Warsaw 1984, after a series of exchanges: *11 ♘xe7+ ♘xe7 12 ♗xe7 ♗xb2 13 ♖b1 ♗c3+ 14 ♔f2 ♗d4+ 15 ♔g3 ♗e5+)* 11 ... e6 12 ♘c7 ♖b8 13 0-0-0. However, in the game Petrosian–Sax, Biel 1985 Black obtained good counterplay after 13 ... b6! 14 ♘e2 ♗b7 15 ♗d6 ♘c5.

    10   ...   **♘d7**
    11   **♗a3**   **b6**
    12   **♘ge2**

And here after 12 ♘d5 e6 13 ♘e7+ ♘xe7 14 ♗xe7 ♖e8 15 ♗a3 ♘c5 Black would have sufficient compensation for the loss of the pawn.

    12   ...   **♗b7**
    13   **♘d5**   **♘de5**
    14   **♘c1**   **e6!**

This move produces new simplifications: Black's positional advantage is strengthened, since White is left with only passive pieces.

    15   **♘e7+**   **♘xe7**
    16   **♗xe7**

White would not profit from an intermediate rook exchange. For instance, 16 ♖xd8+ ♖xd8 17 ♗xe7 ♖e8 18 ♗d6 ♘xc4!

    16   ...   **♖xd1+**
    17   **♔xd1**   **♖e8**
    18   **♗g5**

After Black's forcing moves White is faced with a difficult endgame. In spite of a series of exchanges, Black's initiative does not wane: after the natural retreat 18 ♗a3, the game would have continued: 18 ... f5 19 exf5 ♘xf3! with dangerous threats.

    18   ...   **f5**
    19   **exf5**

    19   ...   **♘xf3!**

This combination could lead into the endgame!

    20   **f6**

The only way to prolong the struggle.

    20   ...   **♘xg5**

20 ... ♗h8 21 h4! would lead to an unclear position.

    21   **fxg7**   **♘h3!**

A paradoxical and very effective reply. When Khalifman, who was under my wardship, returned from the European Junior Championship, already a champion, and showed me his game, I was much impressed by this move and by the entire conduct of Black's plan. Now the Italian master's kingside remains paralyzed to the end of the game.

    22   **♘d3**   **♔xg7**

A remarkable position. Despite the small number of pieces remaining on the board, and material parity, White is completely helpless, and unable to involve his forces in the struggle.

    23   **♔e1**

Hoping to free himself by means of 24 ♘f2.

| 23 | ... | ♖d8 |

Now if 24 ♘f2, the white pawns on the second rank become easy prey for the black rook.

24	♘e5	g5
25	♘g4	h5
26	♘e3	g4!

The pawn advance on the kingside with the knight on h3 looks very effective.

27	♗e2	♘f4
28	♖g1	♖d4
29	♗f1	♘g6
30	♗e2	♘f4

The purpose of the repetition was to gain time on the clock.

| 31 | ♗f1 | ♗e4! |

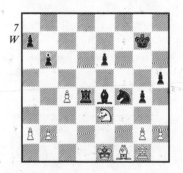

White is in a complete *zugzwang*.

Let us remember that 25 moves ago Black sacrificed a pawn in order to guide the game from the opening into a complex endgame, obtaining for his sacrifice an active rook along the open d-file. This idea is completely vindicated in the endgame, it is sufficient to compare the contestants' rooks: while the white rook is completely out of the game, dragging out a miserable existence on the first rank, his black counterpart virtually controls the whole board. So our original proposition of the interlinking of every stage of the game is implemented in practice.

| 32 | a3 | |

After 32 g3 ♘d3+ 33 ♗xd3 ♗xd3 White cannot avoid material loss.

32	...	e5
33	g3	♘d3+
34	♗xd3	♖xd3
35	♘d1	♗f3

The black pieces are in complete control of the position.

| 36 | ♘c3 | e4 |
| 37 | ♘d5 | e3 |

White resigned.

The close links between the opening stages of the game and the problem of transition from middlegame into endgame can be traced not just in the case of a gambit. Modern opening theory is so deep that it sometimes extends to twenty or twenty-five moves. Contestants often prepare, at home, a plan for transposing from the opening of the game right into the endgame.

Naturally, this applies first and foremost to players of the highest calibre. As an example we follow a game from the deciding match of the World Chess Olympiad at Salonika.

Sax–Yusupov
Salonika 1984

Russian Game

| 1 | e4 | e5 |

2	♘f3	♘f6
3	♘xe5	d6
4	♘f3	♘xe4
5	d4	d5
6	♗d3	♗e7
7	0-0	♘c6
8	♖e1	♗g4
9	c4	♘f6
10	cxd5	♗xf3!

Formerly it was considered that 10 cxd5 prompts the automatic reply 10 ... ♘xd5.

Indeed, attempts have been made in the past to take play into the endgame immediately by means of 10 ... ♕xd5. However, after Kavalek–Toth, Haifa Olympiad 1976, which proceeded: 11 ♘c3 ♗xf3 12 ♘xd5 ♗xd1 13 ♘xc7+ ♔d7 14 ♗f4! ♗g4 15 d5 ♘d4 16 ♘xa8 ♖xa8 17 ♗e5!, no one could be found to try this variation again.

The intermediate exchange on f3 is a modern idea, demonstrated by Smyslov in his Candidates' Match against Grandmaster Hübner.

| 11 | ♕xf3 | ♕xd5 |
| 12 | ♕g3 | |

In Kasparov–Karpov, World Championship 28th game 1984 White chose 12 ♕h3, and after 12 ... ♘xd4 13 ♘c3 ♕d7 transposed play into the endgame despite being a pawn down: 14 ♕xd7+ ♔xd7 15 ♗e3 (*15 ♗g5 deserves consideration*) 15 ... ♘e6 16 ♖ad1.

For the loss of a pawn White has two bishops and beautifully placed rooks on the open files. The game soon concluded with a draw. An immediate queen exchange does not bode well for White. For instance, 12 ♕xd5 ♘xd5 13 ♘c3 (*or 13 ♗e4 0-0-0 14 ♘c3 ♗b4! 15 ♗d2 ♘f6 16 a3 ♘xe4 17 ♖xe4 ♗xc3 18 bxc3 ♘a5 19 ♖ae1 ♘c4, with a better endgame for Black – Ehlvest–Mikhalchishin, Lvov 1984*) 13 ... ♘db4 14 ♗e4 ♘xd4 15 ♗xb7 ♖d8 Timman–Belyavsky, Bugojno 1984.

| 12 | ♕g3 | ♕xd4 |
| 13 | ♘c3 | |

13 ♕xg7? is bad – ♖g8 14 ♕h6 ♘g4. Approximate equality would result on 13 ♕xc7 ♕xd3 14 ♕xb7 0-0! 15 ♕xc6.

Now the threat is 14 ♘b5.

| 13 | ... | 0-0! |

In the aforementioned game between Hubner and Smyslov, Black found himself in a difficult position after 13 ... ♖d8 14 ♗b5.

| 14 | ♘b5 | ♕g4! |

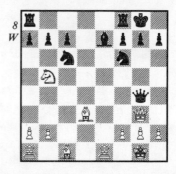

This novelty is the result of well-prepared home analysis. Black transposes play from the opening into the middlegame. White cannot avoid the exchange of queens, since on 15 ♕xc7 there follows 15 ... ♝c5! with dangerous threats.

15 ♛xg4

Perhaps more accurate would have been 15 ♞xc7 ♜ad8 16 ♛xg4 ♞xg4 17 ♝e2! with approximate equality.

15 ... ♞xg4

16 ♝f5

Naturally, it is advisable to drive away the active knight, but 16 ♝e2! deserves consideration.

16 ... ♞f6

17 ♞xc7 ♜ad8

18 ♝e3

The evacuation of the knight from the danger zone through 18 ♞b5 would not succeed in view of 18 ... ♜d5.

18 ... a6!

Cutting off the knight's line of retreat.

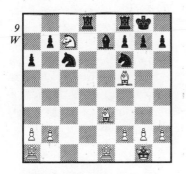

19 ♜ac1?

A serious inaccuracy. Necessary was 19 ♜ed1! (*Weaker is 19 ♝b6 because of 19 ... ♜d2*). For instance 19 ... ♝d6 20 ♝b6 ♝e5 21 ♜xd8 ♜xd8 22 ♞xa6. How can we explain such a blunder, White having so far kept up with his outstanding opponent?

Statistically the number of mistakes committed at the moment of transition from one stage of the game into another, or immediately after such a transition – even into a comparatively simple position – is greater than within each stage. This is explained, above all, by the change in the criteria for evaluating the position. The variation of the Russian game we are examining undergoes a sudden metamorphosis: an explosion occurs in the middlegame but then play passes at once into the ending. While the transition from the opening into the middlegame reveals the strength of active pieces, the transition into the endgame leads to a marked revaluation of what were middlegame criteria. Players attuned to a complex middlegame are often far from ready, psychologically, for such a transformation. In practical play, with only limited thinking time available to players, this psychological factor can be important. In the first place it can lead to time trouble, secondly a player can experience a definite inertia, which takes time to be overcome, often three or four moves. Only after a complete transformation in his thinking is the player fully attuned to the new scale of evaluation. It is precisely within these three to four moves that the majority of mistakes are committed. Naturally, the above applies even more to the cataclysmic transition from opening straight into endgame.

19	...	♗b4
20	♖f1	

Now already bad is 20 ♖ed1 (*or 20 ♖e2*) in view of 20 ... ♗a5, and, because of the weakening of the first rank on 21 ♘xa6, White would be in trouble. 21 ♗f4 ♘b5 would lead to material loss.

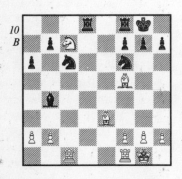

10
B

20	...	♘d4!

As recalled by the captain–trainer of the Soviet team, Grandmaster Makarychev, Arthur Yusupov had to choose between the text move and 20 ... ♗d2, but in the end decided that, for the exploitation of the unfortunate position of the knight on c7, the presence of opposite-colour bishops would not be a hindrance. After 20 ... ♗d2 21 ♗xd2 ♖xd2, 22 ♘xa6 would have been bad in view of 22 ... ♘d4!, but to win the piece would not have been simple, since the d7 and c8 squares were unavailable for the rooks, being under the control of the bishop on f5. Now 21 ... ♘e2+ is threatened, while after 21 ♗xd4 ♖xd4 the white knight would be doomed. Sax tries to complicate the struggle.

21	♖c4	♘xf5
22	♖xb4	♖d7!

An excellent move. 23 ♗f4 does not help now in view of 23 ... ♖c8 24 ♖xb7 ♘d5 25 ♗e5 ♘xc7 26 ♖c1 ♘e8 (Yusupov), while after 23 ♖xb7 the knight falls into a "dead" pin: 23 ... ♘xe3 24 fxe3 ♖c8 25 ♖c1 ♘e8.

23	♖c1	♖c8
24	♖bc4	♖cd8
25	h3	♘xe3
26	fxe3	♔f8
27	e4	♔e7

Beginning to centralize his king. Black's manoeuvre allows White to save his knight, but at the cost of valuable pawns. A transition into a rook endgame by way of 28 ♘d5+ would have been hopeless for White.

28	♖b4	♖d1+
29	♖xd1	♖xd1+
30	♔f2	♔d6
31	e5+	

This move loses quickly.

More stubborn would have been 32 ♔e2, while after 32 ♖xb7 ♔c6 33 ♖a7 ♖d7, again Black would win quickly.

31	...	♔xe5
32	♘a8	

The runaway knight finds rest at last, but where? In the far corner of the board. Again, 32 ♖xb7 is not possible because of the pin 32 ... ♖d7.

32	...	b5
33	a4	♘d5
34	♖b3	bxa4
35	♖b7	♖b1
36	♔f3	a3

White resigned; his knight became exposed in the opening stages of the game, and never got back into play.

In many cases a strategical method of simplification is linked with the achievement of some positional advantage in the opening, which can then be most effectively utilized in the endgame. A spatial supremacy acquired in the opening could serve as such an advantage. The following game illustrates this theme: White, having constrained his opponent's forces, proceeds unhesitatingly to simplify.

His subsequent effective attack in the centre and on the queen's flank shows that, in a transition from the opening into a complex endgame, the position retains its middlegame motifs, where there is plenty of scope for the player's imagination.

Razuvayev–Honfi
Cienfuegos 1976

Sicilian Defence

1	e4	c5
2	♘f3	♘c6
3	d4	cxd4
4	♘xd4	g6
5	c4	♗g7
6	♗e3	♘f6
7	♘c3	0-0

Passive play.

Games played in the last few years show that simplifying by means of 7 ... ♘g4 8 ♕xg4 ♘xd4 facilitates Black's defence.

8	♗e2	d6
9	0-0	♗d7
10	♖c1	♘xd4
11	♗xd4	♗c6

11 ... a6 looks more logical, preparing for b7–b5. However, the text move with the eventual relief of the position is quite often played. White's ensuing play is therefore all the more interesting.

12	f3	♘d7
13	b4!	

White, acquiring space, does not object to the simplifications prepared by his opponent.

In Tukmakov–Velimirovic, Odessa 1975, the indifferent 13 ♔h1 ♗xd4 14 ♕xd4 ♕b6 15 ♕d2 ♘c5 led to an inferior game for White.

13	...	♗xd4 +
14	♕xd4	♕b6
15	♕xb6	♘xb6

The game transposes from the opening into a complex endgame.

16 e5!!

The unexpected beginning of a long combination.

16	...	dxe5
17	b5	♗e8
18	c5	♘d7

19 ♘d5

White's advance on the queen-side creates a highly artistic impression.

19 ...   e6
20 ♘e7+

Firstly, the knight springs into the opponent's camp.

20 ...   ♔g7
21 c6   bxc6
22 bxc6   ♘b6
23 c7

The endgame motif has now clearly emerged – the black forces are tied down by the passed c-pawn.

23 ...   ♗d7
24 ♖fd1

White directs the battle with zeal. Every move creates new threats.

24 ...   ♗a4
25 ♖d6!   ♔f6
26 ♖xb6!   ♔xe7
27 ♖b7

The rook has performed a re-markable manoeuvre: as if on a magic carpet, it flew from the initial f1 square to the key point b7. Now 27 ... ♗d7 would lead to the loss of the bishop after 28 c8(♕) ♖xc8 29 ♖d1, while on 27 ... ♔d6 White intended 28 ♗a6 ♗d7 29 ♖d1+ ♔c6 30 ♖xd7! ♔xd7 31 c8(♕)+.

27 ...   ♔f6
28 ♖cb1!

The pendulum-like motion of this rook on the b1 and c1 squares is fascinating.

28 ...   ♗c6
29 ♖b8   ♖fc8
30 ♖c1!

The ending would have resembled a composition after 30 ... ♗d7 31 ♖xa8 ♖xa8 32 ♗a6 ♗c8 33 ♖b1!

However, the Hungarian Grandmaster preferred a more prosaic move.

30 ...   ♖axb8
31 cxb8(♕)

Although the creation of the passed pawn resulted from a combination started fifteen moves previously, this pawn is finally promoted to a queen, costing Black a piece. The rest of the game is an uncomplicated matter of technique.

31 ...   ♖xb8
32 ♖xc6   ♖b2
33 ♗c4   h6
34 h4   g5
35 hxg5+   ♔xg5
36 ♔h2   ♖b4
37 ♗b3   a5
38 ♖a6   ♖b5
39 ♖a7   ♔f6
40 ♗a4

Black resigned.

The pawn structure emerging in the opening often has an important influence on the whole course of the game. Of great interest are encounters in which one side maps out the contour of the future endgame in the opening stages of the game. The formation of a passed pawn could be a most important factor in such a case; its comparative strength will grow with the elimination of fighting units from the board. The following game played in the Candidates' Tournament of 1953 serves

as a clear example of implemen-
tating a transition into an ending
with a passed pawn.

Euwe–Averbakh
Zurich 1953

Nimzo-Indian Defence

1	d4	♞f6
2	c4	e6
3	♞c3	♝b4
4	e3	0-0
5	♝d3	d5
6	♞f3	c5
7	0-0	♞c6
8	a3	♝xc3
9	bxc3	b6
10	cxd5	exd5
11	♞d2	♝e6
12	♝b2	c4

In this early stage of the game
Black has already chosen a plan
associated with forming a passed
pawn on the queenside. He
relaxes pressure on d4, facilitating
White's thematic continuation
e3–e4.

| 13 | ♝c2 | b5 |
| 14 | f3 | a5 |

Black quickly organizes a
majority attack on the queen's
flank.

15	♖e1	♛b6
16	♞f1	b4
17	♛d2	b3

So, in the transition from the
opening into the middlegame
Black has created an advanced
passed pawn. Now his aim is to
further transpose the game into
the ending, where the pawn will
become irresistible. Naturally,
White has every chance of a

kingside attack, since Black has
used up numerous tempi on the
opposite side of the board. But
one must suffer for the sake of
such a pawn!

18	♝b1	a4
19	e4	♞e7
20	♞g3	♚h8
21	♖e2	♞fg8
22	♞h5	f5!

Certainly a counterattacking
move. Black tries to seize an open
file, which inevitably brings about
the desired simplifications.

23	♛g5	♖f7
24	exf5	♝xf5
25	♝xf5	♞xf5
26	♖ae1	

This move facilitates Black's
task. 26 ♖e5 was necessary, forcing a black piece to defend the d5

pawn and making the subsequent exchanges more difficult to carry out.

26 ... ♛d8!

Grandmaster Averbakh, a brilliant strategist and endgame expert, forces a transposition from the middlegame into the ending, consistently carrying out his plan based on the passed pawn, which was initiated on his 12th move. It is difficult for White to avoid the queen exchange, since the black queen threatens to penetrate to h4.

27 ♛xd8 ♜xd8
28 ♜e8

It can be shown that White himself goes halfway to meet his opponent's plans. Evidently, Euwe, the ex-World Champion, went for the transition into a minor piece ending in order to manoeuvre his knight ♘h5–f4–e6–c5, attacking the black a-pawn. However, even after the recommended 28 ♜e6 the rooks would have been exchanged sooner or later, and the endgame structure would have been unchanged.

28 ... ♜xe8
29 ♜xe8 ♜e7

Yet another forced exchange, otherwise White loses his bishop.

30 ♜xe7 ♘gxe7
31 ♔f2

The only move to stop the decisive entry of the knight ♘f5–e3–d1.

31 ... ♔g8
32 g4

As pointed out by Bronstein, necessary was 32 ♘f4 ♔f7 33 g3 ♘d6 34 ♘g2 ♘b5 35 ♘e3 ♘c8 36 ♘f1 ♔e6 37 ♘d2, and the position could still be held.

Unexpectedly finding himself in an inferior ending, Euwe, trying to move his knight to e6 at any cost, commits a mistake. Even an experienced Grandmaster does not always succeed in switching over instantly to defence after such an abrupt change of course in the game.

32 ... ♘d6
33 ♔e3 ♘b5
34 f4 ♘c8
35 f5 ♘cd6
36 ♘f4

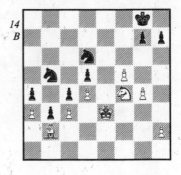

14
B

White has carried out his plan, but an unpleasant surprise awaits him.

36 ... ♘xa3!

Black's strategy has triumphed! The time of the passed b-pawn has arrived!

37 ♗xa3 ♘b5
38 ♗c1 ♘xc3
39 ♘e2 ♘b1!
White resigned

Black's pawn trio is very effective. A remarkably steadfast game.

There are two critical stages in the course of a game: the transition from the opening into the middlegame and from the middlegame into the endgame. The first stage is usually not well defined; its timing is somewhat blurred, since it takes place gradually, by the natural process of mobilizing forces.

In contrast, the transition into the endgame often has a forced, well-defined character and may take place as a result of a decision by one of the players.

Mark Tseitlin–Adamski
Slupsk 1978

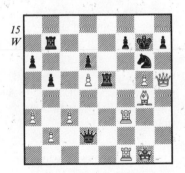

In this complex, double-edged position the game was adjourned. Having accurately evaluated the emerging queen endgame, Tseitlin wrote down his sealed move, which effectively forced the transition into an endgame. In this case the transition from the middlegame is clearly of an explosively instantaneous character.

41	♖xf7+!	♖xf7
42	♖xf7+	♔xf7
43	♕xh7+	♔f8
44	♕h6+!	♔f7

44 ... ♔e7 is bad, in view of ♕g7+.

45	♗e6+	♖xe6
46	dxe6+	♔e7
47	♕g7+	♔xe6
48	♕xg6+	

White does not give the black king a minute's rest. All the black pieces, with the exception of the queens, have been eliminated with the checks. As a result, a complex middlegame has transposed into a technical queen endgame and Tseitlin proceeds confidently to victory.

48	...	♔e7
49	♕f6+	♔e8
50	b4	♕c1+
51	♔g2	

Even while play was still at the middlegame stage, White had to assess how he was going to evade the checks from the hostile queen in the endgame.

| 51 | ... | ♕xa3 |

And White won

A combinative transition from the middlegame into the endgame often occurs not just in an impressive but also in a functional fashion.

Sax–Szell
Hungarian Championships 1984

White has a better pawn structure, but has this any significance when two of his minor pieces are

under attack? Indeed, White's better pawn structure would be unimportant in this case, had he not found an exchange combination.

34   ♕xd4!!   ♕xd4

The queen exchange could have taken place another way: 34 ... cxd4 35 ♗e5 ♕xe5 (*or 35 ... ♔g7 36 ♗xf6+ ♔xf6 37 b4! ♗a6 38 ♘f3 d3 39 cxd3 ♗xd3 40 ♘d4 and Black's pawn weakness would cause difficulties, while a transition into a pawn endgame would be hopeless for Black: 40 ... ♗b5 41 ♘xb5! cxb5 42 g4!*) 36 fxe5 c5 37 ♔g3 c4 38 ♘f3 d3 39 cxd3 c3 40 ♘d4 ♗a6 41 ♔f4 ♗xd3 42 ♔e3 ♗e4 43 g3 and the white knight is clearly stronger than the black bishop.

35   ♗e5+   ♔h7

In the case of 35 ... ♕xe5, White would centralize his knight, controlling all the key squares in his opponent's camp: 36 ♘g6+! ♔g7 37 ♘xe5 ♗b7 38 ♘d7.

36   ♗xd4   cxd4
37   b4

A typical expedient in this sort of ending. White fixes his opponent's pawn weaknesses on the queenside. Black's pawn islands will become easy prey for the white knight. The situation is typical, with a good knight against a bad bishop. The transition into the endgame has transformed White's better pawn structure into a tangible reality.

37   ...   ♗a6
38   ♘xf5   d3
39   cxd3   ♗xd3
40   ♘d4   ♔g6

And, not waiting for his opponent's reply, **Black resigned**.

We have already mentioned that when simplification takes place, in addition to the normal technical problems, there is also a psychological factor, associated with an entirely new type of situation arising on the chessboard. Often one of the players is not quite prepared mentally for such a cardinal change and commits a mistake immediately after the transition.

The complexity of this problem is illustrated by the following example.

Reshevsky–Keres
Zammering 1937

White has acquired a definite advantage in the opening. But how can it be increased? He could proceed with 17 b4, starting a pawn advance on the queen's flank; or possibly he could transfer his queen to the king's flank via c1 and h6 with a subsequent ♘h4 and f2–f4. Reshevsky preferred exchanging

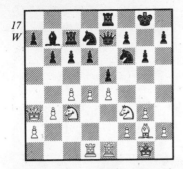

queens, hoping to gain control of the d-file. However, in evaluating the endgame transition, it was necessary to consider other factors. Namely: the black pieces are constrained at the moment, therefore any exchange would favour Black; furthermore, White's weak d4 square would play an even greater role, again in Black's favour, as pieces eliminated from the board. The Estonian Grandmaster succeeded convincingly in exploiting White's mistaken plan. Keres considered the ending of this game as one of his finest creative achievements.

17	dxe5?!	dxe5
18	♕xe7	♖xe7
19	♗h3	♗c8
20	b4	

This is a good example of psychological difficulties arising from an abrupt transition from middlegame into endgame. The assessment of the position, which seemed to be quite unshakeable a few moves ago, has lost much of its significance. The recent plan of attack on the queenside no longer appears so tempting. After the queen exchange the situation has changed, the position which has

emerged could be assessed as approximately equal. 20 ♖e2 with eventual transfer of the knight by the route f3–e1–c2 was worth considering with a doubling of the rooks on the d-file.

20	...	♘f8
21	♗xc8	♖xc8
22	♖d6	♘e8
23	♖d3	f6
24	♖ed1	

White takes control of the d-file, but this does not bring him any particular profit. On the other hand, after the inevitable exchange of rooks, Black is presented with the chance of placing his knight on the dominant d4 square.

24	...	♔f7
25	a4	♔e6
26	♖d8	♖ec7
27	♔f1	♔e7
28	♖8d3	♖d7
29	♖xd7+	♘xd7
30	♔e2	

Black's position is becoming more and more preferable as the exchanges are taking place. After the black knight's move to d6 the weakness of the white pawns on the queen's wing will become evident. It is particularly difficult to defend the c4 square. It is clear that White's action on the queen's flank—20 b4; 25 a4—was unjustified under the changed conditions in an endgame situation. It is tempting for White to establish his knight on d5. However, after 30 b5 cxb5 31 ♘d5+ ♔e6 32 cxb5, the black rook would become dangerously active.

30	...	♘d6
31	♘d2	♘f8

It is instructive to follow the logical way in which Keres carries out his plan of seizing the d4 square.

32	♖a1	♘e6
33	a5	

On a first impression this move gives White sufficient counter-play. The opening of the a-file would suddenly activate the white rook, and if 33 ... b5, the white knight could move on to the cherished d5 outpost.

But ...

33	...	b5!
34	cxb5	♘d4+!

A most important interim check. It was necessary to free the e6 square for the king.

35	♔d3	cxb5

Suddenly it is clear that the apparently excellent position of the white knight on d5 would, in fact, be rather fragile. After 36 ♘d5+ ♔e6, Black could take the centre with f6–f5. Furthermore, Black has an additional tactical idea: ♖c8–c2xd2 and ♘b3+.

36	♖c1	♔e6
37	♘e2	

Again the problem of simplification. Up till now all the exchanges clearly benefited Black. Should he exchange the remaining pair of rooks? What are the guidelines for Black in seeking an answer to this problem? We gives Keres's analysis of the situation: "... Black forces the hostile rook into a passive position, acquiring

opportunities to develop even greater activity for his own pieces. It is interesting to note that the position provides strong points for the knights on both sides – c5 and d5 for White, c4 and d4 for Black. However, the white knights cannot occupy these during the whole course of the endgame, while Black seizes almost ideal positions. *The situation is analogous with regard to the rooks: White must resign himself to defending the b-pawn, while Black has complete control of both open files*". (My emphasis – G.N.).

Now it is clear that the white and black rooks have different destinies, Keres naturally avoids their exchange.

37	...	♘c6!
38	♖b1	♖d8!
39	♔c3	

After 39 ♔e3 ♘c4+! 40 ♘xc4 bxc4 White is helpless. Now that the white king has moved away from e4, Black has an opportunity to undermine the centre.

39	...	f5!
40	exf5+	

White would not be able to hold e4: 40 f3 fxe4 41 fxe4 ♖f8,

and again the black rook would outmanoeuvre its white counterpart, since 42 ♖f1 is impossible in view of 42 ... ♘xe4+.

| 40 | ... | gxf5 |
| 41 | f3 | ♖c8 |

Black sets about besieging the b4 pawn. At first he forces the white king away from it, then transfers the knight by the route ♘d6–e8–f6–d5, having made d5 available with the exchange of the e4 pawn. Keres conducts the ending with logical consistency. Every new manoeuvre is a fresh link in an interesting plan, following a coherent sequence.

| 42 | ♔d3 | ♘e8 |
| 43 | ♘c3 | ♘f6 |

It is clear that after 44 ♘xb5 ♘d5 White could not put up a satisfactory defence to 45 ... ♘xb4+ 46 ♔e2 ♘c3+. For instance: 45 ♖b3 a6 46 ♘a3 ♘cxb4+ 47 ♔e2 ♖c1.

Technique is an integral part of the endgame.

| 44 | ♖b2 | a6 |
| 45 | g4 | |

An interesting offer of a sacrifice in a difficult position. White tries to lure his opponent's forces to the kingside and obtain definite counterplay after 45 ... fxg4 46 fxg4 ♘xg4 47 ♘de4, threatening ♘c5+. But he meets with disappointment:

| 45 | ... | e4+! |

And again tactics come to the aid of strategy. The object of this move is to obtain two pawns against one on the king's flank and, exploiting the remoteness of the white pieces, create a passed pawn.

| 46 | fxe4 | ♘e5+! |

Black's play is based on this intermediate check. Now the e4 pawn is blocked, while the white king is forced to withdraw even further from the struggle.

47	♔c2	fxg4
48	♔b3	♘c4
49	♘xc4	♖xc4
50	♖e2	♔e5
51	♖e1	h5!

A complete triumph for Black's strategy. In spite of material equality, he virtually has an extra piece – the centralized king.

| 52 | ♖d1 | h4 |
| 53 | ♖d8 | g3 |

The black pawns rush on.

54	hxg3	hxg3!
55	♖d3	g2!
56	♘e2	

If 56 ♖g3, 56 ... ♖xc3+! 57 ♔xc3 ♘xe4+ is decisive.

| 56 | ... | ♖xe4 |
| 57 | ♘g1 | ♖e1 |

White resigned.

After studying this endgame, played in a masterly manner by Black, the reader will involuntarily ask the question: could even such eminent chessplayers as Keres and Reshevsky have foreseen and evaluated all the subtleties arising there? Undoubtedly, the answer is no.

The prerequisite is a thorough understanding of the essential process of evaluation in the ending. The basic criteria of evaluation are as follows: the respective positions and the possibility of fast centralization of the kings – except when there are heavy pieces on the board – and the disposition of the pawns, especially the presence, or possibility of creating, a passed pawn. It is essential for chessplayers, in their quest to develop their creative powers, to master the problems of evaluation which inevitably arise from simplification. Alekhine, the great master of combinative play, wrote in the notes to one of his games: "Every chessplayer should try and work out the problems associated with winning the game, fearlessly, before simplifying. To continue to play in a complex position is an extreme measure and should be undertaken only if one cannot find a clear and logical plan."

2　The role of the exchange

The process of chess is based essentially on interlinking exchanges.
　　　　　　　　　　M. Botvinnik

In his final lectures José Raoul Capablanca recalled his long-standing controversy with one of the strongest Grandmasters at the beginning of the century – David Janowski; who said that a well-played game must not reach the endgame. The great Cuban master pointed out that "this mistaken view not only cost him (Janowski) many lost games, but – much more importantly – many weaker players took his words as a revelation."

In modern chess, with the generally higher standard of play and advances in defensive technique, it is rare for a game *not* to reach the endgame. Consequently, Capablanca's sixth commandment is even more topical in our time: "If play is taken into the endgame, decide which pieces it is necessary to retain, and exchange those that are unnecessary."

There is a school of opinion that regards the desire to exchange as an indication of appeasement or fear of the opponent. Such a point of view is disputable, in many cases an exchange or series of exchanges is the shortest way to *win* the game. Throughout the history of chess the skilful use of this strong tactical device – the exchange – was always the hallmark of high-class players.

Sir George Thomas–Alekhine
Baden–Baden 1925

19
B

By means of a series of subtle manoeuvres Black secured a clear positional advantage. The a2 and c3 pawns require constant protection; the weak c4 square can be used by Black as a springboard for his heavy pieces.

| 34 | ... | ♛c4! |
| 35 | ♛xc4 | ♜xc4 |

Aron Nimzowitsch, the brilliant writer of chess literature, describes a queen exchange in his characteristically picturesque way: "It is instructive to note that this exchange arises as a consequence of a simple quest for strategically important squares; it happens, as it were, automatically. The beginner tries to bring about the exchange in other ways: he pursues the wanted piece, but he is unsuccessful; the master occupies the strong points, and the desired exchange falls into his hands like ripe fruit."

The outcome of the game is resolved by a quick centralization of the black king. Before the queen exchange this was impossible.

36 a3   ♗e7
37 ♖fb1   ♗d6!

A characteristic procedure! Alekhine forces his opponent to move his pawns on to black squares, where they are vulnerable.

38 g3   ♚f8
39 ♚g2   ♚e7
40 ♚f2   ♚d7
41 ♚e2   ♚c6
42 ♖a2   ♖ca4

Now that the b5 pawn is protected by the king, Black can create a real threat against the a3 pawn. His opponent's pieces are completely tied down in their efforts to defend the pawn.

43 ♖ha1   ♚d5

A comparison of the position here with that in the previous diagram shows that Black has suc-

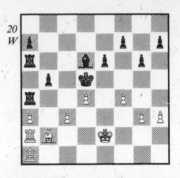

ceeded in realizing his positional advantage. After the exchange of queens, the activity of the black pieces has increased sharply compared with that of the white pieces – including the kings. As the white pieces are obliged to defend the a3 pawn, they lose their mobility and cannot hinder Black's play either on the king's flank or in the centre.

44 ♚d3   ♖6a5
45 ♗c1   a6
46 ♗b2   h5!

Black opens a second front. Because of the threat 47 ... h4, White is forced to place his h-pawn on a black square, which will soon become significant when play shifts to the centre.

47 h4   f6
48 ♗c1   e5!

After this breach White's position collapses.

49 fxe5   fxe5
50 ♗b2   exd4
51 cxd4   b4
52 axb4   ♖xa2
53 bxa5   ♖xb2

White resigned.

The piece exchange, the most universal element of strategy and tactics, is employed at every stage of the game. In the opening, where time is a decisive factor, a tempo-gaining exchange with the object of outstripping the opponent in development can be of great importance. In the middlegame the exchange can be employed for various purposes: the exchange of the opponent's defending pieces to facilitate an attack or, vice versa, the exchange of the opponent's dangerous attacking pieces in organizing one's defence; the seizure of a file or an important strategic square; the creation of weak squares in the opponent's camp or the formation of pawn weaknesses.

The purpose of the exchange in the middlegame can be summarized as an expedient in attaining the best possible disposition of one's own forces in order to resolve a particular strategic or tactical problem.

Rubinstein–Kanal
Rogatska–Slatina 1929

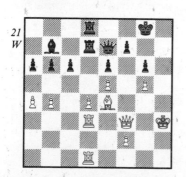

At first glance it seems that White should try and take control

of the h-file, after which his opponent's king would be subjected to attack by White's heavy pieces.

However, an objective analysis of the position shows that this plan cannot be implemented with so much material on the board, since Black's constant pressure along the d-file ties down the white pieces. Furthermore, the d4 and e5 pawns need constant watching. Rubinstein finds an elegant and unexpected solution to the problem. He goes for a queen exchange. This exchange is an excellent illustration of Nimzowitsch's words: "We consider Rubinstein's characteristic quality, the monumental long-term plan, which he uses as a bridge leading from the opening to the endgame."

Indeed, the exchange is the beginning of a well-devised strategy, the purpose of which will become apparent only in the "distant" rook ending.

37 ♕f6!   ♕xf6

An attempt by Black to gain material would result in immediate catastrophe: 37 ... ♕xb4 38 ♔g2! ♕e7 39 ♖h1 ♕xf6 40 gxf6 and he is helpless against the threat 41 ♖dh3.

38 gxf6   ♔h7

After the elimination of the queens, the doubling of the white rooks on the h-file was a real threat, so Black carries out the only available defence against it, provoking the exchange of a pair of rooks.

39 ♔g4   ♖h8

| 40 | ♖h1+ | ♔g8 |
| 41 | ♖xh8+ | ♔xh8 |

After the rook exchange, White's penetration along the open file is no longer a threat, but now he has more important trump cards in hand: an active king and a better pawn structure.

With the exchange of some of the heavy pieces, the criteria for the evaluation have changed. The negative factor of the white king's precarious position has now turned into a position factor – the white king is clearly more active than the black king.

42 b5

The b- and d-pawns have also undergone a mctamorphosis. Whereas in the middlegame they were targets, they have now turned into powerful battering-rams, striking against the hostile pawn formation. It should be noted that in the course of this action White exchanges his active bishop for its passive counterpart. The exchange here is of a temporary nature, its purpose being to distract the enemy rook. White now succeeds in opening a file in the centre; considering that the open position of the black king will become the decisive factor in the game.

42	...	cxb5
43	♗xb7	♖xb7
44	axb5	axb5

More accurate would have been 44 ... a5, though in this case after 45 d5! exd5 46 ♖xd5 ♖a7 47 ♖d6 a4 48 ♖xb6 a3 49 ♖b8+ ♔h7 50 b6 ♖a6 51 b7 ♖b6 52 e6! White wins.

| 45 | d5! | exd5 |
| 46 | ♖xd5 | ♔h7 |

The black king cannot move away from the h-file White strengthens his position methodically.

47	♖xb5	♖b8
48	f4	♔h6
49	♖b1	

Since mate is threatened with 50 ♖h1, Black is forced to allow the white king to enter his camp.

49	...	♔h7
50	♔g5	b5
51	e6!	

The decisive breach.

51	...	fxe6
52	♖h1+	♔g8
53	♔xg6	

Mate in three is threatened: 54 f7+, 55 ♔f6, 56 ♖h8. Black is not saved by 53 ... ♖f8 in view of 54 ♖a1 b4 55 ♖a7 b3 56 ♖g7+ ♔h8 57 ♖h7+ ♔g8 58 f7+.

Black resigned.

The exchange has a distinguished role in attack. Sometimes the exchange with just one enemy defender can immediately decide the battle's outcome.

Lutikov–Kholmov
Semifinal, 23rd Soviet Championship Leningrad 1955

The White king's protection is weak, his queen's position is precarious. The chief defender of the white monarch is the rook: Its exchange decides the game immediately.

22
B

39	...	ℤb1!
40	ℤxb1	♕xb1+
41	♔h2	♗g1+

and **White resigned** in view of the inescapable: 42 ♔g3 ♕d3+ 43 ♔h4 ♗f2+ 44 ♔g5 f6 mate, or 42 ♔h1 ♗f2+ 43 ♔h2 ♕g1 mate.

Exchanges sharply underline the significance of such a factor as a passed pawn, so they are often the shortest way of realizing a positional advantage.

Nesis–Zelinsky
Soviet Correspondence
Championship 1975–1976

23
W

As a result of a sharp opening skirmish, White has an advantage

in development and a strong central passed pawn. However, since this pawn is blockaded, it is not obvious how White should proceed. So it is worthwhile resorting to a well-tried tactical device – exchange – and the solution is simple.

   20   ♘c6!

The queen exchange aggravates the backward development of the black pieces. At the same time, the blockading dark-squared bishop is exchanged.

20	...	♕xb3
21	♘xb3	♗xa3
22	ℤxa3	

It should be noted that the advantage in development is increased through further exchanges of the opponent's active pieces, since this guarantees a real, if temporary, advantage in strength. So, with the disappearance from the board of the queens and a pair of bishops, the more active disposition of the white pieces – it suffices merely to compare the respective mobility of the white and black rooks – becomes even more pronounced.

22	...	g6
23	♘c5	♗c8

This loses immediately, but even after the exchange of White's strong knight at c6 – 23 ... ♘xc6 24 dxc6 ♗c8 – the black pieces are helpless.

24	d6	♔g7
25	♘d4	ℤa7
26	♘b5	

Black resigned.

Quite often a pawn majority on the flank can be exploited only after an exchange of queens, since in this case it is easier to advance the pawns.

Gligoric–Balanel
1956

24
W

White has two bishops and a pawn advantage on the king's flank, but the presence of the queens makes it more difficult to exploit these positional plusses.

White carries out a manoeuvre planned earlier:

    1   ♕g3   ♕xg3

Black does not have any other satisfactory alternatives.

    2   hxg3   ♖d8
    3   f3   g6

More accurate would have been 3 ... h5, slowing down his opponent's pawn advance.

    4   g4   ♔g7
    5   f4

It is precisely the absence of queens that allowed White to advance his pawn army, which is bound to decide the outcome of the battle.

    5   ...   ♖c8

    6   ♖d1!

Gligoric avoids a rook exchange, since a penetration of the white rook on the seventh rank is much more dangerous than a raid by its black counterpart on the second rank.

    6   ...   ♖c2
    7   ♖d7   ♖xg2+
    8   ♔f1   ♖xa2
    9   e6!

With this move White completes his tactical plan and succeeds in forming a dangerous passed pawn.

    9   ...   ♗d5
    10   ♖xf7+   ♔g8
    11   ♖f8+   ♔g7
    12   ♖xe8

White has won his piece back and his opponent is now helpless. The e-pawn will be worth a whole bishop.

    12   ...   ♖c2
    13   e7   ♗c4+
    14   ♔g1   ♗f7
    15   ♖f8

The black rook is unable to stop the passed pawn from the rear, since on 15 ... ♖e2 there follows an unexpected mating finish 16 ♗c3+ ♔h7 17 ♖h8 mate.

The game continued 15 ... g5 16 f5 ♖c4 17 ♔h2 ♖c7 18 ♔g3 h5 19 f6+ and **Black resigned**.

An exchange in the middlegame often serves as a basic element in various combinations.

Ghinda–Gogilea
Romania 1981

    1   ...   ♗xf3!

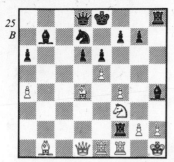

25
B

The exchange of a defending piece, and simultaneous displacement of the g2 pawn from the second rank, is the beginning of an effective mating combination.

2   gxf3   ♖xh2+!!
3   ♔xh2   ♗g3++

Now on 4 ♔g1 there follows ♖h1+! and if 3 ♔xg3, ♛h4 with mate in both cases.

White resigned.

There are numerous examples in which the exchange is the beginning of a positional combination.

Botvinnik–Kan
Sverdlovsk 1943

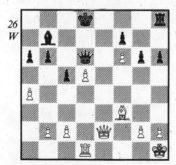

26
W

White has an extra pawn, but it cannot be defended in the normal manner. Botvinnik planned to exchange queens in this position, with the aim of forming connected passed pawns.

In the given case the queen exchange is a tactical device in a combination, based on initiating an attack.

26   ♛e7+!   ♛xe7
27   fxe7+   ♔d7

On 27 ... ♔xe7? there follows the thematic capture of the bishop: 28 d6+.

28   d6   ♗xf3
29   gxf3

With the help of a timely exchange, White retained his material advantage, and he also created *en route* an advanced pawn pair. However, the pawns are blockaded for the time being and the position is a closed one in character; in order to implement his advantage, White has to bring his king into the opponent's camp.

29   ...   ♖c8
30   ♔g2   g5

This impulsive pawn move makes White's problems easier.

31   ♖d5!   ♖g8
32   ♔g3   f6
33   ♔g4   ♔e6
34   ♔h5!

And now Black's weak pawn structure on the king's flank is quite evident.

Naturally, the rook cannot be taken: 34 ... ♔xd5 35 d7, and the pawns are unstoppable.

34   ...   a5
35   ♔xh6   ♔f7

The king has finished his business, having captured yet another pawn, and he can now withdraw.

36   ♔h5   ♖h8+

37   ♔g4   ♖h4+
38   ♔g3

The black rook would demonstrate its ambitious intentions after 38 ♔f5? ♖f4 mate. Now, due to the threat 39 d7, it has to return to its tedious task on the eighth rank.

38   ...   ♖h8
39   f4!

Offering a pawn exchange and opening up the way for the king.

39   ...   gxf4+
40   ♔xf4   ♔e6
41   d7!

A decisive operation, in which the exchange again plays a rôle. A typical procedure – White returns the material and forces a transition into a won pawn endgame.

41   ...   ♔xe7
42   d8(♕)+   ♖xd8
43   ♖xd8   ♔xd8
44   ♔f5

On 44 ... ♔e7, 45 ♔g6! is decisive: 45 ... ♔e6 46 h4 f5 47 ♔g5 ♔e5 48 h5 f4 49 h6 f3 50 h7 f2 51 h8(♕)+!

Black resigned.

In the above extract the queen exchange was employed as a tactical device to accomplish a strategic objective.

We now turn our attention to the opposite case, in which tactics are employed to accomplish an important strategic exchange.

Lputian–Psakhis
Young Masters Championship,
Baku 1979

White, in difficulty, tries to re-

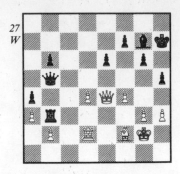

solve all his problems with a central breach.

1   d5   exd5
2   ♖xd5

On the withdrawal of the black queen, White would follow with 3 ♖xh5+, but Black has prepared an unpleasant surprise:

2   ...   f5!

With the aid of this counterblow Psakhis forces a queen exchange and a transition into a favourable endgame.

3   ♖xb5   fxe4
4   ♖xb6   ♖xb2!

It is necessary for Black to exchange rooks for a consistent continuation of his plans. Weaker is 4 ... e3? 5 ♖xb3 axb3 6 ♗xe3 ♗xb2 7 a4 ♗c3 8 ♗c1 with a draw.

5   ♖xb2   ♗xb2
6   ♗c5   ♗c1
7   ♔f2   h4
8   gxh4   ♔g8!

Black plays the ending in a highly technical manner. If 8 ... ♗xf4? 9 ♗e3 ♗d6 10 ♗c1 ♗c5+ 11 ♔g3 and White holds on.

9   h5

In an attempt to delay a swift centralization of the black king,

White gives back the pawn in order to form a counter-distracting passed f-pawn.

9	...	gxh5
10	f5	♔f7
11	♗d4	

Owing to the threat 11 ... ♔f6, this is the only way to retain the passed pawn.

11	...	♗xa3
12	♔e3	♗c1 +
13	♔xe4	a3
14	♔d3	

It seems that White is over the worst, but an exchange again comes to Black's aid – a typical procedure for realizing an advantage in endgames with bishops of the same colour.

14	...	♗g5
15	♔c2	♗f6
16	♗c3	♗xc3

Black secures plenty of time for a win. After 17 ♔xc3 ♔f6 18 ♔b3 ♔xf5, he wins the pawn endgame. **White resigned.**

The exchange has a particularly significant rôle in the endgame, where it can be a vital means of realizing an advantage; it can also serve the opposite purpose, in a difficult situation, of being the only way to save the game. In endgames, when relatively few pieces are left on the board, the disappearance of just one pair of pieces of approximately the same value results in a radical change in evaluating the position.

Romanovsky–Stahlberg
Moscow 1935

We have a heavy-piece end-

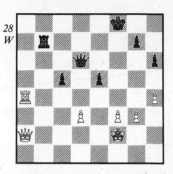

28
W

game on the chessboard. Romanovsky, the well-known Soviet theoretician, has anticipated this type of endgame for the fourth game of the match.

The main criterion in assessing these endings is the whereabouts of the kings. In the given situation neither king is quite comfortable. In this type of position it matters a great deal whose turn it is to move.

| 47 | ♖a8 + | ♖b8 |

A serious and basic mistake. Black is trying to simplify the game when it is precisely in a sharp ending where he could retain equality. A characteristic variation is as follows: 47 ... ♔e7 48 ♕g8 ♖b2 + 49 ♔e1 ♖b1 + 50 ♔d2 ♖d1 +! 51 ♔xd1 ♕xd3 + 52 ♔c1 ♕c3 + 53 ♔b1 ♕d3 + 54 ♔b2 ♕d3 + 55 ♔b3 ♕d3 + 56 ♔a4 ♕d4 + 57 ♔a5 ♕d2 + 58 ♔a6 ♕d6 + 59 ♔b5 ♕d7 + 60 ♔xc5 ♕d4 + and White cannot avoid perpetual check. But now, in a pure queen endgame, the decisive criteria of assessment will be the better pawn structure and greater activity of the white pieces.

48   ♖xb8+   ♛xb8
49   ♛d5

The white queen has occupied a dominating position. Black's best chance is to counterattack. As shown by Romanovsky, after 49 ... ♛c7 50 ♚e3 ♚e7 51 ♚e4 ♚f6 52 h5 – Black falls into a *zugzwang*.

49   ...   ♛b2+
50   ♚e3   ♛c1+
51   ♚e2   ♛c2+
52   ♚e3   ♛c1+
53   ♚e4!   ♛e1+
54   ♚f5   ♛xg3

The white king has managed to escape further checks. Although Black succeeds in exchanging his weak c5 pawn for White's strong g3 pawn, his position has hardly improved.

55   ♛xc5+   ♚g8
56   ♛c4+   ♚h8

More stubborn is 56 ... ♚h7, though even in this case, after 57 ♛e4, White would have good chances of success.

57   ♛g4

An instructive tactical proced-ure. Under the threat of transition into a pawn endgame, the black queen is forced back from its active position.

57   ...   ♛e1

More accurate would have been 57 ... ♛f2 58 ♚xe5 ♛c5+. Now the black king comes under an irresistible attack.

58   ♚g6!   ♛c1
59   ♛d7   ♛g1+
60   ♚f7   ♚h7
61   ♛f5+!   g6
62   ♛d7

and mate is unavoidable.

Black resigned.

So even from the small number of games shown, one can appreciate that at every stage of the game the skilful use of such a powerful expedient as the exchange requires great resourcefulness and a deep penetration into the mysteries of the position.

The basis of the achievement of any objectives is a preliminary accurate assessment of the relative strengths of the pieces in the arising situation.

3 The exchange in the opening

In the opening the rôle of the exchange may seem unimportant. Here the principal aim of the contestants is to mobilize as quickly as possible, and at first glance such an expedient as the exchange does not appear to contribute towards this end. Nevertheless, it would be a mistake to underestimate its importance.

In a whole series of opening variations the exchange of one or another pair of pieces in many respects establishes the subsequent strategies of the middlegame battle, and sometimes even the course of the endgame. This applies especially to opening exchanges whose result is to create organic pawn defects in the opponent's camp.

The Exchange Variation of the Ruy Lopez serves as a typical illustration of this theme – **1 e4 e5 2 ♘f3 ♘c6 3 ♗b5 a6 4 ♗xc6 dxc6**; and, in particular, the Sämisch System of the Nimzo-Indian Defence – **1 d4 ♘f6 2 c4 e6 3 ♘c3 ♗b4 4 a3 ♗xc3+ 5 bxc3**, in which Black intentionally exchanges his dark-squared bishop for the knight to create an important weakness in his opponent's position – the doubled pawns

on the c-file, which can then become a target for counterattack.

Often an exchange is the means by which an important opening objective such as the creation of a powerful pawn centre is realized. Take, for instance, the main variation of the Grünfeld Defence: **1 d4 ♘f6 2 c4 g6 3 ♘c3 d5 4 cxd5 ♘xd5 5 e4 ♘xc3 6 bxc3**.

In the above systems the opening exchanges are undertaken with a view to long-term strategic aims. However, the exchange in the opening is also used to realize a fundamental objective – outstripping the opponent in development.

In discussing the early exchange, one cannot avoid the question of a proper understanding of the time factor, that is, of the theory of tempi.

We quote Tarrasch, the eminent German chessplayer and theorist, regarding the problem of the exchange as applied to one of the variations of the Caro–Kann Defence:

1 e4 c6 2 d4 d5 3 ♘c3 dxe4 4 ♘xe4 ♘f6

"White has outstripped Black in development by two tempi, since he

advanced his pawn and brought out the knight on to the fourth rank; however, this knight is attacked. How should White proceed in order to exploit his advantage in time?

On no account should he exchange knights, for this would be tantamount to losing two tempi: the first one – exchanging his knight, *which has made two moves*, for the black knight, which has made one move; and the second one – exchanging with his opponent's king's pawn . . ."

Naturally, such a strictly arithmetical calculation of tempi cannot be recommended as a basis for deciding whether to go for some or other particular exchange in the opening, but in Tarrasch's somewhat dogmatic approach one can find a grain of reasoning. We simply have to relate this theory to the prevailing circumstances. For instance, should Black exchange knights in the Scotch Game after the initial moves: **1 e4 e5 2 ♘f3 ♘c6 3 d4 exd4 4 ♘xd4**? Naturally, Black should decline the exchange **4 . . . ♘xd4 5 ♕xd4**, not only because the white knight has made an

extra move – that is, "he has lost a tempo" since, according to Tarrasch's theory, any succession of moves with one piece in the opening is a loss of time – but also because of the unpleasant early activation of the white queen, making Black's development difficult.

In his creative games Alekhine took a controversial attitude to the concept of "chess time". Always striving to seize the initiative in the early stages, the ex-World Champion would not count tempi in the opening, though this was not an unconditional assessment. Given objective reasons for it, Alekhine was prepared to lose a tempo in an exchange which would then lead to the opening of the centre and to the supremacy of his pieces along open files or diagonals.

Alekhine–Marshall
New York 1927

The 'New Indian' Defence

1	d4	♘f6
2	c4	e6
3	♘f3	♘e4

This unnatural and time-wasting move is met by an immediate refutation characteristic of Alekhine.

4   ♘fd2!

White also breaks the general rule – "no piece to be moved twice in the opening". However, the text move has an important basis.

A knight exchange would ensure White's seizure of the centre

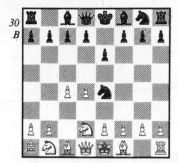

or force his opponent to form a stonewall, which in this position would be disadvantageous for Black.

4 ...   ♗b4

A cunning trap. On 5 a3?, aiming to exchange the minor pieces, there follows 5 ... ♕f6! winning.

5   ♕c2   d5

On 5 ... f5 White would play 6 a3, forcing exchanges and clearly outstripping his opponent in development.

6   ♘c3   f5

Otherwise Black could not hold the centre.

7   ♘dxe4!

Alekhine gave the following comments on this opening exchange:

"After this White easily forces the opening of the central files in subsequent play by means of f2–f3 and, when the opportunity arises, e2–e4. Since he is better developed, this must result in a positional advantage for White."

7   ...   fxe4
8   ♗f4   0-0
9   e3

Threatening 10 a3 with an unavoidable exchange of the dark-squared bishop, otherwise

Black loses the d5 pawn. Black cannot allow such an exchange, since in the absence of its counterpart, White's bishop on f4 would rampage along the dark squares.

9   ...   c6
10   ♗e2   ♘d7
11   a3   ♗e7

As already mentioned, on exchanging his bishop for the knight, Black would be at a disadvantage; he would only exchange his bishop for White's.

12   0-0   ♗g5
13   f3!

When embarking on his exchange operations Alekhine planned precisely this possibility. Now the opening of the centre is unavoidable and White's advantage in development will quickly tell.

13   ...   ♗xf4
14   exf4   ♖xf4

Somewhat more stubborn would have been 14 ... exf3 15 ♖xf3 ♘f6. Committed to a rook exchange, Black concedes the f-file to his opponent without a fight.

15   fxe4   ♖xf1+
16   ♖xf1   e5

Black tries to intensify the battle. White's considerable positional advantage is demonstrated by the variation 16 ... dxc4 17 ♗xc4 ♘b6 18 ♕f2!

17   ♕d2!

White prepares to transfer the queen into an attacking position. In spite of material equality, White has a great positional advantage.

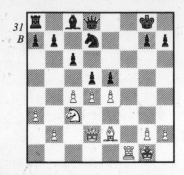

31
B

On 17 ... ♛b6 Alekhine has prepared a positional piece sacrifice: 18 c5 ♛a5 19 exd5 exd4 20 b4! dxc3 21 ♛g5 ♛c7 22 d6 h6 23 ♛e7 and Black is defenceless. The final position is highly colourful and convincing!

17	...	c5
18	dxe5!	d4
19	♛f4!	

White sacrifices his knight with the same objective as in the variation shown above. His queen penetrates the opponent's camp quickly and effectively.

19	...	dxc3
20	♛f7+	♚h8
21	bxc3!	

White's strategy is fully vindicated! Black's pieces are so helpless that it seems as if White has a material advantage. Black plays virtually without a whole flank.

21	...	♛g8
22	♛e7	h6
23	♗h5!	

This move places Black in a *zugzwang*.

23 ... a5

23 ... ♛xc4 loses because of 24 ♗f7 followed by 25 ♛e8+

24	e6	g6
25	exd7	♗xd7
26	♖f7	

Black resigned.

In many opening systems – in particular when the centre is closed – one of the minor pieces, restricted by a pawn chain, often becomes immobile. No wonder there exists the expression "bad" bishop. In these cases the purpose of exchanges in the opening is the liberation of such "bad" pieces. Such tactics are used in a whole series of opening systems.

It is well known that in the French Defence the main disadvantage of Black's set-up is the difficulty of activating his light-squared bishop, restricted by the e6 pawn. In contrast *White*'s light-squared bishop, usually placed on d3, is aiming at Black's kingside.

It is natural that, in many variations of the French Defence, Black tries to exchange the light-squared bishops, since they are so unequal in their prospects.

Konstantinopolsky–Schmidt
3rd Correspondence Olympiad
1958/60

1	e4	e6
2	d4	d5
3	♘c3	♗b4
4	e5	c5
5	a3	♗xc3+
6	bxc3	

The opening exchange of bishop for knight in this system of the

French Defence bears Nimzo-witsch's name. In order to coun-teract a distinct weakening of the black squares on his kingside, Black disrupts his opponent's pawn structure with the help of this thematic exchange, widens the field of action and adds a dynamic, double-edged dimen-sion to the struggle.

6 ...   ♛c7

7 ♛g4

The mobilization of their queens identifies by and large the contestants' plans. White tries to exploit the disappearance of Black's dark-squared bishop from the board and to organize an at-tack on the king's flank, while the black queen surveys the pawn weaknesses on the c-file.

7 ...   f5

8 ♛g3   cxd4

9 cxd4   ♞e7

10 ♝d2   0-0

11 ♝d3

This bishop has taken up an excellent position and Black's subsequent move prepares to exchange the light-squared bishops.

11 ...   b6!

12 ♞e2   ♝a6

The same exchange manoeuvre was played in the famous game between Reshevsky and Botvin-nik in their World Championship game in 1948.

13 ♞f4   ♛d7

14 h4

White chooses the most accur-ate sequence of moves, as recom-mended by Keres. The attempt to win a tempo by means of 14 ♝xa6 ♞xa6 15 ♛d3 would give Black the opportunity of carrying out an important defensive man-oeuvre: ♞a6–c7–e8.

14 ...   ♝xd3

15 ♛xd3   ♜c8!

An interesting idea: after the exchange of light-squared bishops Black has gained control of the c4 square and the king's rook heads for it. The struggle becomes tense.

16 ♜h3   ♜c4

17 ♜g3   ♞bc6

18 c3   ♜f8

19 ♚f1

Otherwise it would be difficult to bring the other rook into the attack. Simplifying on the king's flank with an exchange combi-nation would turn out to be in Black's favour: 19 ♞h5 ♞g6 20 ♞xg7 ♛xg7 21 h5.

19 ...   ♜f7

20 ♜e1   ♛c8! (33)

We can now sum up Black's opening strategy. With the help of an exchange of bishops he obtained adequate counterplay on the queenside. After the

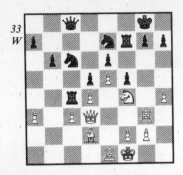

33
W

double-edged complications the game came to a peaceful conclusion.

We now examine a game in which an exchange in the opening was undertaken in conjunction with a far-reaching strategic plan.

Fischer–Gligoric
Havana Olympiad 1966
Ruy Lopez

1   e4   e5
2   ♘f3   ♘c6
3   ♗b5

This active entry into the scene of the light-squared bishop was studied more than four centuries ago by the Spanish priest Ruy Lopez, and to this day it remains one of the most important themes in opening theory.

The attacking possibilities of the light-squared Spanish bishop are well-known; many generations of black kings have laid down their lives under its great power. It seems strange, therefore, that even great chessplayers part with this bishop at the very beginning of the game, without

any obvious reason, exchanging it for the knight. Could this exchange indicate a tacit offer of a draw? But then why is it that the Exchange Variation of the Ruy Lopez has been in the arsenal of such uncompromising fighters as Emmanuel Lasker and Bobby Fischer?

3   ...   a6
4   ♗xc6!

Fischer gives an exclamation mark to this move. His high estimation of this exchange lies in its psychological effect. As a rule Black, having made preparations to play the Ruy Lopez, is attuned to a more complex battle. There is an amusing story on this subject, told by Bronstein. A day before one of the rounds of the Soviet Championships in Kiev, his opponent suggested transferring the game, with the agreement of the umpires, to the second row, a little further from the auditorium. The offer was accepted. And here are Bronstein's remarks the following day: "In answer to 1 e4 I calmly played 1 ... e5. So, it is to be the Spanish Game. But suddenly, what do I see? The bishop takes my knight on c6. My mood deteriorated in an instant, I was in anguish. What can one say? The move ♗xc6 is not at all bad; was it made as a consequence of the commotion caused by transferring the game to the quiet second row? Hardly. It was not difficult for White to play for a draw, since the noise there was like the Niagara Falls.

"Reluctantly, I played a defensive game. *It is quite difficult to play in this type of position, mainly because there are little prospects in it.*" (My emphasis – G.N.) The last phrase eloquently explains the psychological significance of the exclamation mark placed by Fischer after the move 4 ♗xc6.

A similar incident occurred in the historic encounter between Lasker and Capablanca, St. Petersburg 1914.

4 ...   dxc6

In the case of 4 ... bxc6 White provokes yet another opening exchange with the d-pawn: 5 d4 exd4 6 ♕xd4, clearly outstripping his opponent in development and seizing the initiative.

5   0-0

This move is the beginning of a variation attributed to Barendreht, the Dutch master, though it was also played by Ed. Lasker. Commenting on this game, Fischer's rival, Gligoric, the eminent Yugoslav Grandmaster, gives the following, pure-chess appraisal of the variation: "Although White exchanged his strong bishop for the knight, his strategic plan cannot be faulted. He has won a tempo for development (the exchange with regard to the time factor), spoiled Black's pawn configuration (the exchange with the aim of achieving strategic objectives) and renewed the threat against the e5 pawn (the exchange with the aim of creating concrete threats)."

5   ...   f6

The safest continuation.

If 5 ... ♕d6, the following variation deserves consideration: 6 d3 f6 7 ♗e3 ♗e6 8 ♘bd2 c5 9 ♕e2 ♘e7 10 c3! Dvoretsky–Romanishin, Vilnius, 1975. A sharp battle would develop on 5 ... ♗g4 6 h3 h5!? One also encounters the move 5 ... ♕e7, as in the game between Dvoretsky and Smyslov, Odessa 1974, which is likewise a good illustration of our theme. The game continued as follows: 6 d4 exd4 7 ♕xd4 ♗g4 8 ♗f4.

White allows his knight to be exchanged, despite a weakening of the pawns protecting his monarch. Topping his bill – a lead in development, at any price. A concrete, well-founded approach to the position is needed, since Black's move *5 ... ♕e7* has made it more difficult for him to mobilize his kingside forces. 8 ... ♗xf3 9 gxf3 ♘f6 10 ♘c3 ♘h5 Since White's queen's bishop would become dangerous in the middlegame and even more so in an endgame, Black must exchange it, though this takes time. 11 ♗g3 ♖d8. A different order of moves would not entirely solve the problem: *11 ... ♘xg3 12 hxg3 ♕c5 13 ♖ad1 ♕xd4 14 ♖xd4 ♗c5 15 ♖d3 ♔e7 16 ♖fd1*, and White has a stable advantage in the endgame (Gaprindashvili–Bohosjan, Tbilisi 1974). 12 ♕e3! This retreat is stronger than *12 ♕a4 ♘xg3 13 hxg3 ♕b4* (Bednarski–Smyslov, Olympiad 1972). 12 ... ♘xg3 13 hxg3 ♕c5 14 ♖ad1 ♕xe3. Black would not succeed in equalizing the position with *14 ... ♖xd1 15 ♖xd1 ♗d6 16 f4*. In the inevitable ending it will become evident that the defect in Black's pawn structure is significant. So in spite of simplifications the advantage in development is still appreciable. 15 ♖xd8+ ♔xd8 16 ♖d1+ ♔c8 *16 ... ♕d4 17 ♖xd4+ ♔e8* came under consideration. Now the black king cannot stop the pawn advance in the centre. 17 fxe3 g6. More accurate was *17 ... ♗b4*. 18 e5 ♗g7 19 f4 f6 20 exf6 ♗xf6 21 e4.

34
B

White is virtually playing with an extra pawn. It is not difficult to see that the consequences of the exchange 4 ♗xc6 have lasted into the endgame. 21 ... h5 22 ♔g2 ♗xc3 23 bxc3 b5 24 e5 a5 25 ♔h3! b4 26 ♔h4 ♖e8 27 ♔g5 ♖e6 28 ♔h6. 1-0.

6 d4   ♗g4

The escalation of opening exchanges demands accurate play from Black. So, in the game between Fischer and Portisch, playing in the Havana Olympiad, there followed: 6 ... exd4 7 ♘xd4

c5 8 ♘b3 ♕xd1 9 ♖xd1 ♗d6 *(better is 9 ... ♗g4 10 f3 ♗e6)* 10 ♘a5! b5 *(After 10 ... ♗g4? Black can rely only on a co-authorship in the opening formation 11 f3 0-0-0? 12 e5! Hort–Zheliandinov, Havana 1967)* 11 c4 ♘e7 12 ♗e3 f5 13 ♘c3 f4 14 e5! and White's superior development quickly became decisive.

7 c3

In the exchange variation a gambit is also possible but, if Black accepts it, his opponent acquires a menacing initiative: 7 ... exd4 8 cxd4 ♗xf3 9 ♕xf3 ♕xd4 10 ♖d1 ♕c4 11 ♗f4.

7 ...   exd4

And here it would have been better to refrain from the exchange by means of 7 ... ♗d6.

8 cxd4   ♕d7
9 h3   ♗e6

A serious inaccuracy. Naturally, it is tempting to keep aiming at the h3 pawn, but it is considerably more important to maintain the pin and the pressure in the centre by means of 9 ... ♗h5.

Now White's hands are free.

10 ♘c3   0-0-0
11 ♗f4

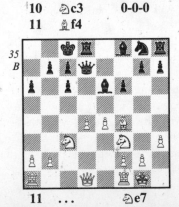

35
B

11 ...   ♘e7

It was imperative for Black to rectify his backward development as quickly as possible. This problem could have been resolved more energetically by exchanging the dark-squared bishops: 11 ... ♝d6! 12 ♗xd6 ♛xd6. As pointed out by Fischer, an attempt to intercept the initiative forcibly would have failed: 11 ... g5!? 12 ♗g3 h5! 13 d5 cxd5 14 ♖c1!

For instance: 14 ... ♝d6 15 ♘a4! ♚b8 16 ♘c5 ♛e7 17 ♘xa6+! bxa6 18 ♘d4 ♝d7 19 ♛b3+ ♚a7 20 ♖xc7+! ♝xc7 21 ♗xc7 ♝b5 22 ♘c6+! ♝xc6 23 ♛b6+ with mate next move. White wins even more effectively in case of 14 ... dxe4 15 ♘a4! ♚b8 16 ♖xc7! ♛xd1 17 ♖c8+!! ♚a7 18 ♗b8+ ♚a8 19 ♘b6 mate. A problem-like finish!

Digressing from the brilliant analysis of the American Grandmaster, we note that Black's attempt at active counterplay is refuted since White's opening was built on sound strategy. Beginning with the move 4 ♗xc6, he played for a lead in development and, in spite of material equality, acquired a dynamic advantage in strength, whereas Black was doomed to play defensively.

12	♖c1	♘g6
13	♗g3	♝d6
14	♘a4	♗xg3

14 ... ♚b8 was necessary, so that after 15 ♗xd6 Black would have had time for 15 ... cxd6, not only correcting his pawn configuration but stopping the white

knight occupying the key square c5.

15	fxg3	♚b8
16	♘c5	♛d6
17	♛a4	♚a7?

Black, clearly unable to bear the strain arising unexpectedly from the drawish Exchange Variation, does not find the correct response 17 ... ♝c8.

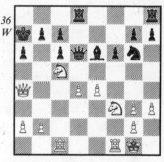

36 W

| 18 | ♘xa6! | ♝xh3 |

The last hope. In case of 18 ... bxa6 19 ♖xc6, with Black suffering heavy losses.

19	e5!	♘xe5
20	dxe5	fxe5
21	♘c5+	♚b8
22	gxh3	

and **Black** soon **resigned**.

The above miniature reflects well the problems for both players in the Exchange Variation of the Ruy Lopez – the purely chess problems as well as the psychological ones.

To say that 4 ♗xc6 is stronger than the usual 4 ♗a4 is not corroborated by any specific variations; and yet, after the Bronstein experience, we can only quote Ed Lasker's words: "A change of variation is an important expedient in chess – we make constant use of it."

So this exchange can be recommended to chessplayers attracted to endgames, who believe that it is sometimes worth giving up the king's bishop for a better disposition of pawns.

It is well known that ex-World Champion Mikhail Botvinnik devoted enormous attention to opening preparation. Throughout his creative life he showed a dynamic and objective approach to the opening. In his rich store of openings there were numerous systems where exchanges formed basic links with subsequent strategic ideas.

Ragozin–Botvinnik
Leningrad 1940

Grünfeld Defence

1	d4	♘f6
2	c4	g6
3	♘c3	d5
4	♗f4	♗g7
5	e3	0-0
6	♖c1	c5
7	dxc5	

This variation became very popular after Capablanca–Reshevsky, Amsterdam 1938. It was well known that after the usual 7 ... ♕a5 8 cxd5 ♖d8 White obtains an advantage with 9 ♗c4. In preparation for the above game, Botvinnik found an interesting opportunity for counterplay associated with the exchange of his dark-squared bishop.

7	...	♗e6
8	♘f3	♘c6
9	♕a4	♘e4
10	♗e2	

White cannot exchange his opponent's active knight, since after 10 ♘xe4 dxe4 he loses his b2 pawn. He prefers therefore to finish his development. However, a surprise is in store for him.

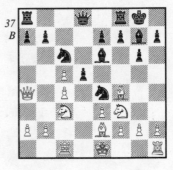

10	...	♗xc3+

We quote Botvinnik's comments to this far from obvious move:

"It was not easy to decide on this move, since Black parts with his excellent bishop; but an objective analysis confirms the correctness of this exchange. Eliminating his opponent's knight on c3 and retaining his own centralized knight, Black acquires a great advantage in the centre, which should be advantageous in subsequent play."

The objective decision of the opening exchange, linked with the problem of centralizing a piece and with the general strategic plan of action, is characteristic of Botvinnik's play.

11 bxc3   dxc4

It is clear that the white c5 pawn is doomed, since 12 ♗xc4 ♘xc5 13 ♕b5 ♗xc4 14 ♕xc5 (*14 ♕xc4 ♘d3+*) 14 ... ♕d3 15 ♘g1 ♖ad8 leads to mate; the black knight's life is expensive. In Botvinnik's opinion White should have castled. It was necessary to give up the c5 pawn and to finish his development: 12 0-0 ♘xc5 13 ♕b5 ♕a5 14 ♗xc4 ♕xb5 15 ♗xb5 ♗xa2.

12 ♘d4   ♗d5

Black centralizes his pieces systematically. Now 13 0-0 is bad, in view of 13 ... e5 14 ♘xc6 ♗xc6, and two of White's pieces are attacked.

13 ♗h6   ♖e8
14 0-0   e5

This move has two immediate threats: 15 ... exd4 and 15 ... ♕h4.

15 ♘f3   ♘xc5
16 ♕b5

Let us sum up the results of the original exchange 10 ... ♗xc3+. Black has an extra pawn and could simplify by means of 16 ... ♕a5 17 ♗xc4 ♕xb5 18 ♗xb5 ♗xa2. However, since he has full control of the centre, he has nothing to fear in the ensuing complications.

16 ...   b6
17 ♖fd1   a6
18 ♕b1   b5
19 ♗g5   ♕d7

It is interesting that Botvinnik considers this move is already decisive. Indeed, in spite of his pin

on the black bishop, White cannot prevent the pawn advance ... e5–e4, since after 20 e4 there follows 20 ... ♗xe4! 21 ♖xd7 ♗xb1 22 ♖d5 ♘e4 23 ♖xb1 ♘xc3 and Black acquires a large material advantage.

20 a4   e4
21 axb5   axb5
22 ♘d4   ♘xd4
23 exd4   ♘b3

Evidently Black has achieved overwhelming superiority. However, the game continued till the time control:

24 ♕c2 ♘xc1 25 ♕xc1 ♖a2 26 ♕e3 ♕c6 27 h4 f6 28 ♗h6 ♖ea8 29 ♔h2 ♖b2 30 ♗g4 b4 31 cxb4 c3 32 ♖c1 c2 33 f3 ♖b1 34 fxe4 ♗xe4 35 d5 ♕d6+! Accuracy to the end; the d5 pawn is poisoned: 35 ... ♕xd5 36 ♖xc2 or 35 ... ♗xd5 36 ♕e7 ♗f7 37 ♗f3. **36 ♗f4 ♕xb4 37 ♗e6+**

White would not succeed in utilizing the strength of his two bishops by means of 37 ♖xc2 ♗xc2 38 ♕e6+ ♔g7 39 ♕d7+ ♔h8 40 ♗h6, in view of 40 ... ♖h1+ 41 ♔xh1 ♕e1+ 42 ♔h2 ♕xh4+.

37 ...   ♔h8 38 d6 ♖xc1 39 ♕xc1 ♕d4 40 d7 ♗c6.

White wrote down his sealed move, **41 h5**, but **resigned** without resuming play.

It has already been mentioned that in the Nimzo-Indian Defence the problem of the opening exchange is the cornerstone of a series of variations. In this respect it is interesting to examine a classic exchange initiated by Flohr in

the second game of his match
against the young Botvinnik.

Flohr–Botvinnik
match 1933

Nimzo-Indian Defence

1	d4	♘f6
2	c4	e6
3	♘c3	♗b4
4	♕c2	

This variation, popular in the
thirties and forties, was advocated
by Alekhine.

4	...	c5

Together with 4 ... d5 this
move is also popular today.

5	dxc5	♘a6
6	g3	

An unfortunate decision.
Stronger is 6 a3 ♗xc3+ 7 ♕xc3
♘xc5 8 f3, which leads to the
Krauz Variation, named after the
Danish theorist. In fact, the sixth
game of the same match continued in accordance with the line
given in up-to-date reference
books: 8 ... d6 9 e4 e5 10 ♗e3
♕c7 11 ♘e2 ♗e6 12 ♕c2! and
after a series of exchanges White
obtained a slightly better game.

6	...	♕a5

Practically forcing the queen
exchange, since on 7 ♗d2, ♕xc5
is strong.

7	♗g2	♗xc3+
8	♕xc3	

The correct decision! It may
seem paradoxical but, precisely
after the queen exchange, White's
pawn weaknesses on the queenside will become less of a disadvantage. The point is that the

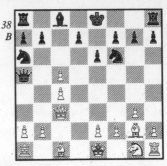

38
B

piece most dangerous to White's
c-pawns is removed from the
board and White's advantage in
development becomes more appreciable.

8	...	♕xc3+
9	bxc3	♘xc5
10	♗a3!	

A very important manoeuvre.
White prepares to exchange his
bishop for the knight in order to
close the c-file and improve the
security of his weak pawns: 10 ...
♘ce4 11 ♘f3! ♘xc3 12 ♖c1 ♘a4
13 ♘d4, and Black is unable to
complete his development.

10	...	d6
11	♘f3	♘fe4
12	♖c1	♗d7

It is important for Black to
retain a piece on the c5 square, as
in the case of 12 ... b6 White
succeeds in closing the c-file with
the following exchanges: 13 ♘d2
♗b7 14 ♘xe4 ♗xe4 15 ♖xe4
♘xe4 16 f3 ♘c5 17 ♗xc5 dxc5,
with a draw.

13	♘d2	♘xd2
14	♔xd2	♖c8
15	♗xc5	♖xc5

Black succeeded in retaining his
outpost with a piece, but at the
cost of the b7 pawn.

16	♗xb7	♖xc4
17	♖b1	♔e7
18	♗f3	♖a4
19	♖b2	♖c8

Obviously Black has the better pawn structure, but this is not enough to win in the four-rook ending.

20	♖a1	♗c6
21	♗xc6	♖xc6

Draw

Not surprisingly, one can find many fine examples of opening exchanges in the creative games of ex – World Champion Vasily Smyslov, another outstanding chessplayer of our times.

Smyslov's games are always distinguished by their lucidity, their sharp style, together with a jewel of an endgame technique. Many of his games are virtually engraved with the motto – through simplification to victory.

Smyslov–Stolz
Bucharest 1953

Nimzo-Indian Defence

1	d4	♘f6
2	c4	e6
3	♘c3	♗b4
4	e3	d6
5	♘e2	c5
6	dxc5	dxc5
7	♕xd8+	♔xd8

At the very beginning of the game White has exchanged queens. The purpose behind this is significantly more aggressive than it first appears. Within a few moves the black king, deprived of

castling, finds himself in a dangerous situation. It should also be noted that Smyslov succeeds in exploiting the uneasy foothold of the black bishop on b4.

8	♗d2	♔e7
9	♘f4	b6

The positional threat 10 ♘d3 was unpleasant, but now the black bishop is completely cut off.

10	a3	♗a5

Black avoids exchanging his bishop, since after 10 ... ♗xc3 11 ♗xc3 the white bishop becomes very active. However a tactical surprise awaits him.

11	b4!	cxb4
12	axb4	♗xb4
13	♘cd5+	♘xd5
14	♘xd5+	exd5
15	♗xb4+	

Despite further simplifications, the black king unexpectedly comes under fire. For instance, 15 ... ♔e6 16 cxd5+ ♔xd5 17 ♗e2 ♗f5 18 ♗f3+ ♗e4 19 ♖d1+.

15	...	♔f6
16	cxd5	

Though there is material equality on the board, White's advantage in development and the

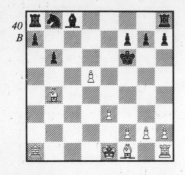

40
B

exposed position of the black king are clearly crucial. However, all these dynamic factors could become of less consequence in the approaching endgame, so White has to play with inventiveness and energy.

16	...	♗b7
17	♗c3+	♔e7
18	♗b4+	♔f6
19	0-0-0!	

White is not afraid of shadows! Well-advised to mobilize his reserves as quickly as possible, the king castles without pawn cover.

19	...	♗a6
20	♖d4	h5
21	♔b2	♗xf1

A rare case of exchanging with the king's bishop on its original square, but Black's plan is entirely logical. He must complete his development, hoping that his queen-side pawn majority will come into its own.

22	♖xf1	♘a6
23	♗c3	♘c5!

Black would be glad of exchanging the dangerous bishop, even at the cost of losing a pawn:

24 ♖g4+ ♔e7 25 ♖xg7 ♘a4+ 26 ♔b3 ♘xc3 27 ♔xc3 ♔f6, after which he has a good chance of salvation in a four-rook endgame.

24 e4!

No simplifying now. Black's king is under threat; he must retain his attacking forces and avoid exchanges.

24	...	♖hc8
25	f4	a5
26	f5	

Systematically depriving the black king of retreat squares. Occupation of the weak e5 square by White's bishop can wait.

26	...	b5
27	d6	

White would now benefit from further simplifications, since after 27 ... ♘a4+ 28 ♖xa4+ ♖xc3 29 ♔xc3 bxa4 30 ♔d4 ♖e8 31 e5+ ♖xe5 32 d7 the pawn becomes decisive.

27	...	♔g5
28	e5	♔h6

Again, 28 ... ♘a4+ is bad in view of 29 ♖xa4 bxa4 30 ♗d2+ ♔g4 31 ♖f4+ ♔g5 32 d7 and the passed pawn cannot be stopped.

29	d7	♖d8
30	e6!	fxe6
31	fxe6	♘xe6
32	♖d6	

and **Black** soon **resigned**.

It can be shown that exchanges in the opening stages of the game affect even such initially constrained pieces as the rooks. As a rule, rook exchanges occur at the end of the middlegame or in the endgame. However, to every rule there is an exception.

Chiburdanidze–Alexandria
Women's World
Championship, 7th game
Borzhomi–Tbilisi 1981

Bird's Opening

1 g3   d5
2 f4   h5!?

Nowadays we seldom see such an original sequel to the first move, yet this is still tried by eminent chessplayers.

3 ♗g2   h4
4 ♘c3   c6
5 d3   hxg3

So the problem of a rook exchange has arisen already.

It seems that 5 ... ♕b6 would have been more flexible, maintaining the possibility of a later rook exchange. The h-pawn could be useful in the variation 6 ♘f3 h3!, causing development difficulties for White on the kingside, whereas in the case of 6 ♘a4 ♕a5+ 7 c3 ♘f6, the rook

exchange would be more profitable for Black, as it could be used in an attack against his opponent's king.

6 hxg3   ♖xh1
7 ♗xh1   ♕b6

After the rook exchange this thrust does not have so much force; since White's hands are untied she can proceed to mobilize her pieces.

8 ♘f3   ♗g4
9 ♘a4   ♕a5+
10 c3   ♘d7
11 ♗e3   ♘h6
12 b4   ♕c7
13 ♘c5   ♗xf3

A dubious move. The other exchange should have been considered: 13 ... ♘xc5 14 ♗xc5, and instead of eliminating White's knight Black could have restrained it by means of 14 ... f6. After the exchange, the World Champion acquires the advantage of the two bishops. However, Black retains some prospects owing to the white king's risky position.

14 ♗xf3   ♘f6
15 ♕a4   ♘f5
16 ♗f2   e5!

Nana Alexandria, Candidate for the Women's crown, truly reflects in her style of play the aggressive Georgian school of chess.

17 g4   ♗xc5
18 bxc5   ♘e7
19 fxe5   ♕xe5
20 ♕d4   ♘g6
21 ♖b1

No single art critic or commen-

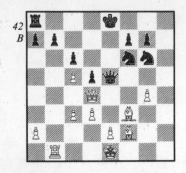

tator can penetrate the essence of a work of art as profoundly as its creator. To a large extent this holds true for the art of chess. Alexandria is well known to Soviet chessplayers not only as a brilliant, highly gifted player, but also as an interesting journalist, a sincere and frank critic of her own games. We shall therefore quote from her own words; they are of particular interest to us as the problem of the exchange has a prominent place in them: "The game swung in Black's favour on the 13th move, when the important bishop was exchanged for the knight" (*So it may appear from within! But from the vantage of an unbiased observer, this move must be viewed with distrust*). "White has two bishops and control of the b-file but, pushing against pawns, lacks space; the white king is insecure. So the position is approximately equal."

21 ...   ♛xd4?

This queen exchange was criticized unanimously.

Black's unusual play in this game would have been ratified by the logical 21 ... 0-0-0. How does Nana herself explain her last move? "Black obviously became alarmed and went into an inferior endgame. It was necessary to castle, after which it is not obvious how White could have mounted an attack." Indeed, after 21 ... 0-0-0 22 ♛b4 ♜d7, the attacking chances would have been on Black's side. And if White exchanges queens, then after 22 ♛xe5 ♞xe5, her bishops would be obliged to give themselves up for the black knights, otherwise the white pawn islands fall victim to black pirates.

22 ♝xd4   0-0-0
23 ♚d2   ♞d7

Alexandria writes: "At first glance the exchange of the g7 for the c5 pawn appears suspect. The last move ws played with the idea f7–f6 at an opportune moment, creating a fortress."

A transition to trench warfare by means of the other exchange: 23 ... ♞h4 24 g5 ♞xf3+ 25 exf3 ♞e8 is clearly not to Black's taste; and an attempt to exploit the open h-file would not succeed: 23 ... ♜h8 24 g5 ♞e8 25 ♝g4+ ♚c7 26 ♜f1 ♜f8 27 ♝h5! with two overwhelming white bishops.

24 ♝xg7   ♞xc5
25 ♜h1   ♞d7
26 ♜h5   ♜e8

26 ... ♜g8 would have been consistent – 27 ♝d4 f6, in which case it is difficult for White to break through.

27 ♝d4   ♚c7

And here 27 ... f6 should have

been considered, since White can- not take the a7 pawn: 28 ♗xa7 b6 29 ♖h7 ♘gf8 and the bishop is lost.

| | 28 | ♖f5 | ♖e7 |
| | 29 | ♗f2 | |

More accurate would have been the immediate 29 g5, stopping 29 ... f6; but Black fails to grasp this opportunity.

| | 29 | ... | ♘de5 |
| | 30 | g5 | ♘xf3+ |

A typical time pressure exchange, after which the white kingside pawns acquire kinetic energy.

In such positions the female World Champion gives her opponents no chance whatsoever. The game continued as follows: **31 exf3 ♖d7 32 ♖f6 ♘f8 33 f4 b6 34 ♗d4 c5 35 ♗e5+ ♔d8 36 f5.** White's advantage is overwhelm-

ing, and after **36 ... ♔e8 37 ♖h6! ♖d8 38 ♖h8 f6 39 ♗xf6 ♖d6 40 ♗g7 Black resigned**.

There is a whole series of opening systems, with many variations, in which forces are arranged with the intention of exchanging off one or other of the opponent's important defenders. A striking example, in the Yugoslav Attack of the Dragon Variation of the Sicilian Defence, is White's attempt to exchange dark-squared bishops.

It is well known that from the exchange of the fianchettoed bishop there arises a whole knot of weak squares, which facilitates the storming of the king's fortress. Evidently such exchanges occur in the moment of transition from opening into middlegame, and we shall examine this problem next.

4   The exchange in the middlegame

Mark Dvoretsky, the well-known Soviet chess trainer, correctly observed: "In their comments regarding the opening stages of their games, chessplayers often refer to a very important game played with the same variation, which influenced them in choosing that particular opening. Such references are far less common when we come to the middlegame ..."

Indeed, it is more difficult to play the middlegame in accordance with set patterns. Decisions are taken as a result of one's natural creative resources. This is precisely why it is much more difficult to study the process of play in the middlegame than in the other stages of the game. And yet, in spite of the difficulties of generalizing about the numerous methods and devices used in the middlegame – for instance, regarding the pawn structure – they can be classified and studied.

Would it not be possible to apply Dvoretsky's observation to a study of such a widely-used middlegame expedient as the exchange?

Botvinnik–Petrosian
World Championship, 14th game
Moscow 1963

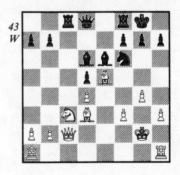

43
W

Commenting on Black's last move 17 ... ♗e7–d6, Botvinnik pointed out that the exchange of dark-squared bishops in the given situation was a precondition for an endgame profitable for White; he drew the reader's attention to a game played twenty-four years earlier.

What was it that stimulated such a remote association? Let us turn to Botvinnik's comments.

"The character of the struggle arising in the given pawn configuration after the exchange of dark-squared bishops is well known to me, by reason of the similarity with the Levenfish–Kotov game (11th Soviet Championship Leningrad 1939), in which I was helping Ragozin as a commentator. White will be at an advantage in the endgame, since his pieces will be more active than those of his opponent."

Levenfish–Kotov
11th Soviet Championship
Leningrad 1939

Despite important differences in the disposition of the pieces, Botvinnik's astonishing strategic acuity suggested an identity of evaluation, nearly a quarter of a century after the original game was played.

Levenfish proceeded:

14   🗝e5

White wishes to bring about the exchange in circumstances most favourable to himself.

14   ...   f6

Black, not wanting to concede the e5 square, has, however, weakened his kingside.

15	🗝xd6	♛xd6
16	♛c2	g6
17	♘b5	

In the case of the tempting sacrifice: 17 🗝xg6 hxg6 18 ♛xg6+ ♚h8 19 🗒e3 ♛d7! Black could set up a satisfactory defence.

17	...	♛d7
18	♛e2	♚f7!

As pointed out by Ragozin, this is already the only satisfactory move. If 18 ... 🗝f5 19 🗝xf5 ♛xf5 20 ♘c7 ♘xc7 (*20 ... 🗒c8 also loses in view of 21 ♘e6! 🗒xc1 22 🗒xc1 🗒f7 23 ♘d8*) 21 🗒xc7+, the threat of 22 ♛e7 is decisive.

19	♛d2	a6
20	♛a5	🗒c8

Black, in an extremely constrained situation, naturally tries to exchange pieces; but White does not evade simplifications. The point is that White will have a small but steady advantage in the endgame.

21	🗒xc8	♛xc8
22	♘c3	♛c7
23	♛xc7	♘xc7

This is the ending Botvinnik remembered when defending his title in the match against Petrosian. And now it becomes clear that the resemblance between the two games does not just involve a similarity of pawn structure.

24	♘a4	🗝d7
25	♘c5	🗝c6
26	🗒c1	🗒c8

27	h4	♘b5
28	♗xb5!	♗xb5

Let us remember this exchange.

White is striving for an ending in which his knight will be more active than his opponent's bishop.

| 29 | ♖c3 | b6 |

White now forces a transition into a minor-piece endgame in which Black will have no easy defence.

| 30 | ♘a4 | ♖xc3 |
| 31 | ♘xc3 | |

45
B

The struggle in this ending, lasting for more than 40 moves, concluded with victory for White despite opportunities for Black to save the game. Prospects of a similar ending occurred to the then World Champion in the original position shown in *43*. That game continued:

18	♖ae1	♗xe5
19	♖xe5	g6
20	♕f2	♘d7
21	♖e2	♘b6
22	♖he1	

So, as in the original game, White does not force events and has no objection to simplifying.

| 22 | ... | ♘c4 |
| 23 | ♗xc4! | |

Botvinnik writes: "Now White remains with a good knight against a bad bishop." A familiar motif!

| 23 | ... | ♖xc4 |

Bad is 23 ... dxc4, in view of 24 d5! ♗d7 25 ♕d4 with overwhelming superiority for White.

24	♖d2	♖e8
25	♖e3	a6
26	b3	♖c6
27	♘a4	

We already know of this knight manoeuvre from the Levenfish–Kotov game.

27	...	b6
28	♘b2	a5
29	♘d3	

White activates his knight to the maximum, while Black is unable to mobilize his bishop.

29	...	f6
30	h4	♗f7
31	♖xe8+	♗xe8

Simplification does not lessen Black's difficulties. On the contrary, the disparity in the activity of the minor pieces becomes more perceptible.

32	♕e3	♗f7
33	g5	♗e6
34	♘f4	♗f7

The black bishop is unable to further its prospects. On 34 ... ♗f5 there follows 35 gxf6 ♖xf6 36 ♕e5!

35	♘d3	♗e6
36	gxf6	♕xf6
37	♕g5!	

By analogy with the remembered game, White strives to

reach the same material relationship: rook and good knight
against rook and bad bishop, with
similar pawn structures.

| 37 | ... | ♛xg5+ |
| 38 | hxg5 | |

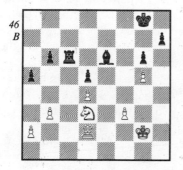

We should pause in this situation, as here the analogy between
the two exchange ideas is demonstrated, and the present realization of an advantage in this ending is also related to our theme.
White, consenting to exchanging
minor pieces at the appropriate
moment, wins a pawn in the process. This is a typical example of
transforming one advantage into
another in the course of simplifying.

38	...	a4
39	bxa4	♜c4
40	a5!	bxa5
41	♘c5	

The white knight has been trying for a long time to reach the
important square c5, but the opportunity presented itself only
after the pawn exchange.

| 41 | ... | ♝f5 |

Though at last Black succeeds
in activating his unlucky bishop,
the quick centralization of the
white king is decisive.

42	♔g3	a4
43	♔f4	a3
44	♔e5	♜b4
45	♘d3	

White has no objection to the
exchange of the minor pieces, as
this would result in winning a
pawn.

45	...	♜b5
46	♔d6	♔f7
47	♔c6	

The white monarch swiftly penetrates his opponent's camp and
Botvinnik forces a transition into
a rook endgame, winning a pawn
en route.

47	...	♝xd3
48	♜xd3	♜b2
49	♜xa3	♜g2
50	♔xd5	♜xg5+
51	♔c6!	

The game passed into a rook
ending with an extra pawn for
White and, in spite of technical
difficulties, Botvinnik succeeded
in exploiting his material advantage.

We have already observed that
one of the most difficult problems
of the middlegame is the problem
of choice. The question of
exchanging a piece – or avoiding
the exchange – is of particular
relevance in this respect. What are
the guidelines of a true master in
making his decision?

We illustrate this theme by examining a contest between two of
the most outstanding chessplayers
of our time, availing ourselves of

the comments of Grandmaster Karpov.

Karpov–Spassky
6th Sports Meeting of the Soviet People Riga 1975

47
W

Before the game has even emerged from the opening stages White has to decide whether to make an exchange that is clearly middlegame in character. Karpov writes: "Should White exchange knights? On the one hand, reducing the number of pieces would help Black to defend a somewhat constrained position. On the other hand, if the game is taken into a position where Black has hanging pawns, White's opportunities for an initiative will be enhanced in the presence of the greater number of pieces on the board. Consequently, the choice is a matter of style."

However, it becomes clear on White's tenth move that the problem bears not just a strategic but a concrete character.

   9   0-0   ♞d7

   10   ♞xd5

"Now that the queen's knight has established its position, White should exchange."

So the then World Champion examines not just the advisability of the exchange in general terms, but gives a concrete reason for his decision, as depending on such an apparently slight factor as the position of the queen's knight.

   10   ...   exd5

After 10 ... ♗xd5 11 e4, White would have the opportunity to form a dynamic pawn centre.

   11   ♖d1   ♞f6

   12   ♞e5

This move threatens to exchange one of Black's bishops with 13 ♞c6; therefore the advance of the black c-pawn is forced.

   12   ...   c5

   13   dxc5

White has no doubts regarding this pawn exchange, since he now acquires a great deal of space for his pieces and the chance of applying active pressure against his opponent's pawns. At the same time, Black is in a dilemma— should he play with hanging pawns (after 13 ... bxc5) or go for a position with an isolated pawn. Spassky, the ex-World Champion, chooses the second course, as more in keeping with his active style.

   13   ...   ♗xc5

   14   ♞d3!

The threat of the exchange forces Black to withdraw his bishop. The point is that after 14

... ♖c8 15 ♘xc5, the formation of hanging pawns by way of 15 ... bxc5 would be entirely to White's advantage in view of 16 ♗g5, and in the absence of the black bishop their defence would be fraught with difficulties.

14 ...   ♗d6

15 ♗f4!

The pursuit of the bishop continues.

Karpov writes: "The exchange of the dark-squared bishops is one of White's best plans, since it makes the isolated d5 pawn even more vulnerable." A classic example of the theme "the exchange – to attack the isolated pawn."

15 ...   ♖e8

16 e3   ♘e4

17 ♗xd6   ♕xd6

18 ♘f4   ♖ac8

Even after the better 18 ... ♖ad8, White would have a clear advantage.

19 ♕a4   ♕e7!? (48)

Considering that in the normal course of events this position would be untenable, Spassky tries to sharpen the struggle with an obscure threat against the white king. The capture of the a7 pawn appears risky, but White takes up the challenge. In leading to this crucial decision, the question of an exchange has been in the forefront.

20 ♕xa7

"I thought for quite a long time over this move and satisfied myself that it would give me an advantage. It seems that the queen

leaves the critical battle zone, but on a closer examination it becomes clear that it can *quickly be exchanged* for its black counterpart" (my emphasis–G.N.). We singled out specifically these words of the then World Champion, to emphasize once again the importance of the actual exchange, or its possibility, in the course of a sharp game.

20 ...   ♘xf2

21 ♘xd5   ♗xd5

22 ♕xe7

After the natural 22 ... ♖xe7 23 ♖xd5 ♘g4 24 ♗h3 ♘xe3 25 ♗xc8 ♘xd5 26 ♖d1, the sum total of exchanges would lead to a bad endgame for Black. Spassky prefers to give up his queen, hoping that in the ensuing dynamic imbalance White will encounter difficulties.

22 ...   ♘xd1

23 ♖ac1!

An effective *intermezzo*; White now seizes the open c-file, since Black clearly cannot exchange rooks; 23 ... ♖xc1 24 ♕xe8 mate.

23 ...   ♖b8

24 ♕b4   ♗xg2

| 25 | ♔xg2 | ♘xe3+ |
| 26 | ♔h1 | ♖e6 |

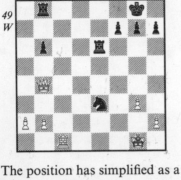

49
W

The position has simplified as a result of a series of exchanges, but it is too early to speak of an endgame. In the given situation the question is how to realize a material advantage in the middlegame. What is the rôle of the exchange in such a situation? Karpov answers the question with great insight: "The material balance is completely in White's favour. Insofar as the battle can continue on either flank, the queen is stronger than a rook and a knight. Black's chances for a draw are linked to the unsatisfactory position of the white king. If Black manages to improve the coordination of his pieces, the realization of White's advantage would become more difficult. White therefore begins a forcing variation, the purpose of which is to exchange one of the black rooks; in the event, his opponent's resistance will sharply diminish."

So we may already infer from this game that the exchange in the middlegame, as in the endgame, is one method of realizing a material

advantage, since it can neutralize the opponent's tactical opportunities.

27	♕f4	♖d8
28	♕d4	♖de8
29	♕d7	

Exploiting the weakness of the eighth rank, White forces a rook exchange.

| 29 | ... | ♘g4 |
| 30 | ♖c8! | |

This terrible pin deprives Black of the possibility of organizing a counterattack. After 30 ... ♖e1+ there follows 31 ♔g2 ♖e2+ 32 ♔h3 ♘f2+ 33 ♔h4 ♖e4+ 34 g4 and if 34 ... ♖xg4+, then 35 ♕xg4! wins.

30	...	♘f6
31	♖xe8+	♖xe8
32	♕b7	♖e6
33	♕b8+	♘e8

After the rook exchange the realization of the advantage is a matter of technique. Evidently the outcome of the game will be decided by a pawn march on the queen's flank.

34	a4	g6
35	b4	♔g7
36	♕b7	h5
37	♔g2	♔f6
38	h3	♖d6
39	a5	

White, having improved his position, now continues to advance his pawns.

39	...	bxa5
40	bxa5	♖e6
41	a6	♘c7
42	a7!	

Precise. Such a pawn is worth more than a knight.

42	...	♜e7
43	♕c6+	♚e5
44	♚f3	

Black is in *zugzwang*. On 44 ...
♚f5 White wins with 45 ♕c5+
♚f6 46 ♕d6+. **Black resigned**.

So we may come to some conclusions. A true master has a wide range of resources at his disposal, enabling him to decide on the advisability of the exchange: his methodology being a mental comparison of the game being played with one he has played beforehand, with similar positional features; an objective appraisal of the situation arising after the exchange; and even making use of such psychological factors as the creative power and style of his opponent.

In modern times there is no human activity that has not been systematized. Chess too has not escaped this "lucky" fate. As a result of such systemization, the "Encyclopaedia of Chess Openings" was produced, based on exhaustive opening classifications and detailed indexing; and, similarly, universal reference books on various aspects of endings were published. A similar work for the middlegame would be more complex. The middlegame, the most creative and original phase of chess, resists straightforward classification by its very nature.

In spite of the fact that the general strategic problems and tactical elements associated with the middlegame are well known, the problem of their systematization has been taken up comparatively recently.

An attempt to subdivide the material into columns, based on one of the most important middlegame expedients – the exchange – is fraught with serious methodological difficulties.

The exchange is the most widely used idea in the middlegame, with the most diverse objectives. It can be as useful in attack as in defence. It can lead to an abrupt simplification of the position, or it can play the first chord of a complicated combination. The middlegame exchange can be the shortest and safest way to realize a material advantage, and may help to strengthen a positional one.

Moreover, all of these motifs are entwined, like a tangle of electric wire.

Notwithstanding the above difficulties, we shall try to isolate the basic strategic moments pertaining to our theme:

A. The exchange – (the shortest way of) realizing material advantage.
B. The exchange in attack and defence, and the exchange as an integral part of the combination.
C. Realizing a positional advantage with the aid of the exchange.

Such a classification is quite conventional; readers can satisfy themselves from the games we examine later in this chapter of the interrelationship of various aspects of the exchange and of the diverse strategic and tactical problems which can be resolved with its help.

Realizing a Material Advantage

We have already noted that the reasons for an exchange in the middlegame can be very diverse, be it the exchange of a defending or attacking piece, for the seizure of strategically important squares or for the opening of files. All such motifs are encountered in the realization of a material advantage.

Alekhine–Kostic
Bled 1931

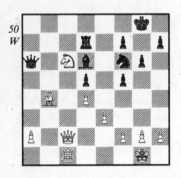

Though White has an extra pawn, the black pieces are quite active.

In this middlegame position we follow Alekhine's method of realizing material advantage.

27   ♞b8!

An effective move, forcing the exchange of queens and one pair of minor pieces.

27   ...   ♝xb8

Alas, Black is forced to exchange his strong dark-squared bishop, a principal defender!

28	♕c8+	♕xc8
29	♖xc8+	♚g7
30	♝f8+	♚h8
31	♖xb8	

Accomplishing these exchanges heightens the significance of White's passed pawn. Moreover, now that its opposite number has been eliminated, the white bishop is clearly stronger than the black knight.

31	...	h5
32	♝d6+	♚h7
33	♝e5	♞g8

Following the exchange of bishops, the weakness of the dark squares has become so appreciable that, despite the paucity of material remaining on the board, the black king's position is alarming, and the only way to avoid mate is by making this unattractive knight-move.

34	h4	f6
35	♝f4	♖a7
36	♖b5	♞h6

White's task is facilitated by this move. The a2 pawn should have been captured.

37   a4!

Profiting from the fact that the black rook cannot abandon the seventh rank in view of ♖b7+, White quickly pushes his passed pawn.

37	...	♘f7
38	a5	♘d8
39	♗b8!	

The active bishop is successful everywhere. All of this is a consequence of White's profitable exchange of the minor pieces. Playing on both flanks, the bishop is clearly stronger than the knight.

39	...	♖d7
40	a6	♘c6
41	♖b6	

White can now permit the exchange of his powerful bishop. In the ensuing rook endgame the advanced a-pawn decides the outcome of the game.

41	...	♘xb8
42	♖xb8	♔h6

The threat of a rook exchange with the transition into a pawn endgame compels the black king to take up an extremely open position. At the same time its white counterpart, after the necessary preparations, soon moves over to the queenside to support the passed pawn.

43	♖b7	

Forcing away a piece of the same value by threatening to exchange – a typical device in the majority of endings: the black rook must abandon an important square and the white infantry becomes extremely dangerous.

43	...	♖d6
44	a7	♖a6
45	f4	♖a2
46	♔f1	g5
47	g3	

Black, virtually in *zugzwang*,

cannot stop the white monarch's passage f1–b1–b8. **Black resigned.**

Timman–Larsen
Montreal 1979

With his last move **46 ... c5** Bent Larsen attacked the hostile queen.

How should White proceed: retain the queens, trying to exploit the insecure position of his opponent's king – for example, 47 ♕b8+ ♔d7 48 ♕g8 – or force a transition into a minor-piece ending?

The Dutch Grandmaster chooses the quickest way to victory, making use of the absence of pawn cover for the black king, he deprives his opponent of the slightest chance of counterplay.

47	♕c4!	♕xc4

Forced, otherwise Black loses yet another pawn.

48	♗xc4	♘e8
49	♔f3	♔c7

At this stage the game was adjourned. As in the previous example, the bishop operating on two flanks is clearly stronger than the knight.

50	a5	♘d6
51	♗d5	♔b8
52	♔f4	♔a7

The black king has to be content with the walk-on part of blocking the dangerous passed pawn at the edge of the board, while its white counterpart dominates centre.

| 53 | ♔e5 | ♘b5 |
| 54 | ♗c4 | |

An immediate approach to the kingside would rather complicate matters; for instance, 54 ♔f5 ♘c3 55 ♗b3 ♔a6

| 54 | ... | ♔a6 |
| 55 | ♔d5 | |

At this point it would be possible to transpose into a queen endgame by way of: 55 ♗xb5+ ♔xb5 56 ♔d5 c4 57 a6 c3 58 a7 c2 59 a8(♕) c1(♕) 60 ♕b7+, but it is much simpler to realize the material advantage in the minor-piece ending.

55	...	♔xa5
56	♔xc5	♘c3
57	♗d5	♘d1
58	f4	♘f2

The black knight creeps to the rear of the kingside. But what can it do on its own against the opponent's king and bishop? To the very end of the game the black monarch will just be an observer of the knight's heroic but fruitless efforts.

| 59 | ♔d4! | |

The pawn cannot be taken, since on 59 ... ♘xh3 the knight would pay with its life for only one pawn.

| 59 | ... | ♔b4 |

Bad is 59 ... ♔b6 60 ♔e3 ♘d1+ 61 ♔d2 ♘b2 62 ♗b3 and the knight has fallen into a trap.

60	♗f3	♘xh3
61	♔e3	g5
62	f5	g4

As pointed out by Timman, the game would also have been lost after 62 ... ♔c5 63 ♗g4 ♘g1 64 ♔f2 h5 65 ♗xh5 ♘h3+ 66 ♔f3!

| 63 | ♗xg4 | ♘g5 |
| 64 | ♔d4! | |

Once again stopping the approach of the enemy king.

| 64 | ... | ♔b3 |
| 65 | ♗h5 | |

and after a few moves **Black resigned**.

Frequently the stronger side gives up a material advantage to obtain specific benefits.

Yates–Alekhine
San Remo 1930

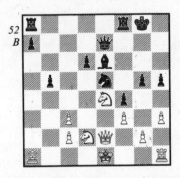

As a result of passive opening play, White was left with the worse position and then lost a pawn. Subsequently Black forced a minor-piece exchange and occupies the permanent c4 square with his knight, from where it applies pressure both on the queenside and in the centre.

32	...	♗ c4
33	♘xc4	♘xc4
34	♖ d1	♕e5
35	♕d3	♖ f5
36	0-0	

53
B

Taking into account that his own king is unprotected, Alekhine gives back his extra pawn with the help of a little combination. In this transaction he exchanges queens and a pair of rooks, after which the negative factor of his king's precarious position will no longer be relevant.

36	...	d5!
37	♕xd5+	♕xd5
38	♖xd5	♖xd5
39	♘f6+	♔f7
40	♘xd5	♖ d8
41	♘b4	♖ d2

Compare this position with that shown in the previous diagram. Despite material equality, Black has a definite positional advantage. His remaining pieces are actively placed and cooperate well. A beautiful example of transforming a material into a positional advantage!

54
W

If now White plays 42 ♖f2, then after the rook exchange the black a-pawn would win.

42	♖a1	a5
43	♘c6	♖xc2
44	♘xa5	♘e3

The situation is now very favourable for Black.

Black needs to retain his knight since it cooperates beautifully with the rook, while the disconnected white pieces are unable to defend their kingside.

The game continued: **45 ♖b1 ♖xg2+ 46 ♔h1 ♖g3 47 ♘c6 ♖xh3+ 48 ♔g1 ♖g3+ 49 ♔h2 ♔f6 50 ♘d4 g4 51 fxg4 ♘xg4+ 52 ♔h1 f3**, and after a few moves **White resigned.**

Smyslov–Botvinnik
World Championship, 12th game
Moscow 1957

Black, employing a novelty in the Sicilian Defence, was striving for this position. At first glance he has adequate compensation for the loss of a pawn. White's c-pawns are weak, the e4 pawn is under attack; if he protects them with 11 ♘d2 there follows 11 ...

Ξxd2! 12 ⌂xd2 ⌂xe4+ and 13 ... ⌂xc5. After 11 ♗d4, 11 ... ⌂xd4 12 ⌂xd4 ⌂xe4 13 f3 ⌂xc3 is possible.

11   ⌂d4!

Smyslov, at that time the challenger for the world crown, does not defend his central pawn, but attacks a key defender, the knight on c6, provoking an exchange.

This knight exchange highlights the weakness of the black queenside pawns, and the white bishop on c5 takes aim at the a7 pawn.

11   ...   ⌂xe4
12   ⌂xc6   bxc6
13   ♗xa7

Let us evaluate the position. White has two bishops and a passed pawn on the a-file; Black is deprived of realistic counterplay. The knight exchange has shifted the balance in White's favour. Here we need to emphasize once more that the basis of an objective, rational exchange is to evaluate accurately the dynamic balance of the pieces in the situation arising.

This also applies to pawns: the a7 pawn was more valuable than the e4 pawn. The point is that the elimination of the apparently insignificant pawn on the queen's wing, in anticipation of the approaching endgame, was in White's favour. Now, with the support of the two bishops, nothing prevents the white a-pawn from becoming a monster.

13   ...   ♗f5
14   f3

Offering to give back the pawn with 14 ... ⌂xc3, but then 15 ♗b6 Ξd7 16 a4 with the extremely unpleasant threat of 17 g4 and 18 ♗a5, winning the knight.

14   ...   ⌂d6
15   a4   Ξa8
16   ♗b6   0-0
17   c5   ⌂c8
18   g4   ♗e6
19   a5   ⌂xb6
20   cxb6

Black exchanges his passive knight for the active bishop, but now White has two connected passed pawns. Strictly speaking, this exchange was virtually forced, otherwise Black would have been in *zugzwang*. We have an example here of transforming one type of positional advantage– having the good bishop against the bad knight – into another– having connected passed pawns.

20   ...   Ξfb8

Black succeeds in winning back a pawn with this move and restoring material equality, but in the process one pair of rooks is exchanged and Black's remaining rook will have to struggle against the passed b-pawn. As shown by Smyslov, White could win quickly by the elegant 21 ♗f2! ♖xb6 22 axb6 ♖xa1 23 b7 ♖b1 24 ♗a6! ♖b2+ 25 ♔e3 ♔f8 26 ♖d1 ♔e8 27 ♖d4 c5 28 ♖b4!

After White's text move his task is more difficult.

21	♗d3	♖xb6
22	axb6	♖xa1+
23	♔d2	♖a2+

Naturally, after 23 ... ♖xh1 24 b7 ♖xh2+ 25 ♗e2 Black cannot prevent the b-pawn from queening.

24	♔e3	♗c8
25	♖d1	♖b2
26	♗c4!	

Enabling the white rook to penetrate to the eighth rank.

26	...	♔g7
27	♖d8	♗e6

A typical tactic – transposing the game into a rook ending, which is well-known for its drawing tendencies. But in this particular case the exchange of the minor pieces does not bring any relief to Black, the party responsible being Vasily Smyslov's meticulous technique. We note that the b-pawn could have been captured, but at too costly a price: 27 ... ♗b7 28 ♖d7 ♖xb6 29 ♖xe7, and Black cannot defend the f7 pawn.

28	♗xe6	fxe6
29	♖b8	e5
30	c4	♔f7
31	c5	♔e6
32	♖d8!	

The b-pawn has been quasi-promoted from a simple passed pawn to a defended passed pawn, and the white rook is now free to perform a more gratifying rôle, cutting off the enemy king from the queenside and then safeguarding the entry of White's own monarch into the hostile camp.

The game continued:
32 ... g5 33 h3 ♖b1 34 ♔d2 ♖b5 35 ♔d3 ♖b1 36 ♔c4 ♖c1+ 37 ♔b4 ♖b1+ 38 ♔a4 ♖a1+ 39 ♔b4 ♖b1+ 40 ♔a3 ♖a1+ 41 ♔b2 ♖a5 42 ♖d3. The threat of transposing into a pawn endgame is decisive: **42 ... ♖a8 43 ♔b3 ♖a5 and Black resigned.**

Taimanov–Smyslov
Moscow–Leningrad Match 1968

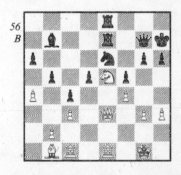

56
B

There are never any compromises between those traditional rivals – Moscow and Leningrad. Taimanov sacrificed a pawn for the initiative, but Black defended precisely, retaining his material advantage. Moreover, the position of the white king appears rather suspect.

However, in view of the position's closed character, realizing these advantages requires an unusual decision on Black's part:

31 ... ♘g5!
Ingeniously played!

Once more the exchange plays an important rôle. The text move is not just a straight offer to exchange knights by way of 32 fxg5? ♖xe5 with definite advantage; the point is that Black practically forces the exchange of the four rooks and a pair of knights, creating threats against the white king and at the same time winning yet another pawn. What more can be asked for from just one move?

32	g4	♖xe5
33	fxe5	♖xe5
34	♕b6	

The rook cannot be taken because of 34 ... ♘f3+, and after 34 ♕g3 there follows 34 ... f4 35 ♕g2 d4 with an overwhelming attack.

34	...	♘f3+
35	♔f2	♘xe1
36	♖xe1	♖xe1
37	♔xe1	

Evidently Black has profited a great deal from these exchanges. Black having seized all the strategically important squares, the white king's position is hopelessly weakened.

37	...	♗c8
38	axb5	axb5
39	♕xb5	

If 39 gxf5, then 39 ... ♗xf5 40 ♗xf5 ♕e5+ 41 ♔d1 ♕xf5 and Black wins the queen endgame.

| 39 | ... | ♕e5+ |
| 40 | ♔d1 | fxg4 |

White resigned.

In exploiting a material advantage in the middlegame, the exchange of a piece – or a series of forced exchanges – may lead to an immediate conclusion of the game. We saw this in the previous example. The same theme reappears in the following position. It is interesting to observe that this time the exchange, occurring, as it were, behind the scenes, still has a decisive effect on the main drama.

Konstantinopolsky–Tolush
Moscow 1950

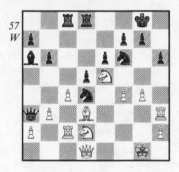

21   g5

In the preceding sharp battle White has sacrificed his d4 pawn, hoping to destroy the black king's protective pawn screen with a swift pawn attack.

21   ...   dxc4!

Black does not retreat the attacked knight, but starts a strong counterattack. 21 ... ♘xc2 is bad, in view of 22 gxf6 with a decisive attack.

But now 22 gxf6 is followed by 22 ... cxd3 23 ♕g4 ♘f5 with a clear advantage for Black. Here we have a case of a threatened exchange! White prefers to give up his rook for a knight and retain his strong d3 bishop.

22   ♖xc4   ♗xc4

23 bxc4 ♕c5!

In spite of a considerable material advantage, Black must play with precision to repulse White's attack.

White's last move was a red flag for Tolush to counterattack.

24 gxf6 ♘e2++
25 ♔h1 ♘xf4
26 ♕g4 g5
27 ♘df3 ♖xd3

With the loss of the powerful bishop, White's position is hopeless.

28 ♘xd3 ♘xd3
29 ♕h5 ♕f2

White exceeded his time limit. **0–1**

We now consider an example in which the exchange of queens turns out to be the shortest way of exploiting a material advantage.

Timman–Kavalek
Montreal 1979

58
B

Black has an extra pawn but, due to White's advanced passed pawn, and the presence of queens, this material advantage is difficult to exploit.

36 ... ♕f3!

An excellent move, forcing an exchange with the active white queen.

After the elimination of queens White is deprived of any chance of counterplay – the loss of the d7 pawn is only a matter of time.

37 ♕xf3

37 ♕xe5 is answered by the decisive 37 ... ♗b7!

37 ... ♖xf3
38 ♘c4

What else is left for White? On 38 ♘d3 ... ♖xd7 39 ♘xe5 ♖xd2 40 ♖xd2 ♖xb3. Moreover, he has precious little chance of saving the game in a rook ending – his pawns are too weak.

38 ... ♗xc4
39 bxc4 ♖c3
40 ♖e1 ♖xc4
41 ♖xe5 ♔f7

The game was adjourned here. Black has a won endgame. The final moves were as follows: **42 ♖d3 ♖xa4 43 ♖f3+ ♔g6 44 ♖e7 ♖d4 45 ♖ff7 ♖g8 46 ♖f4 ♖xf4 47 gxf4.** On 47 ♖e8 ... ♖d4! is decisive. **47 ... ♖d8 48 ♖e6+ ♔f5. White resigned.**

In complex, dynamic positions, fraught with tactical elements, the exchange – more accurately, the decision regarding its expediency – should be undertaken with the utmost caution, only after verifying several times the opponent's possible replies.

In all games, players are constantly faced with the problem of exchanging pieces and pawns. The problem has a critical cost for the player with the material advantage: he must decide on the dynamic balance that best realizes this.

On the other hand, the player with a material deficiency tries in good time, as early as the middlegame, to arrive at a situation which would be favourable for a draw at the end of the game.

The above considerations are well illustrated in the following game.

Bondarevsky–Suetin
Moscow 1950

24   ♘e6!

Black expected the more obvious 24 ♘xb7, when he intended 24 ... ♘d6! White would then have had to choose either to give back a pawn or, after 25 ♘xd6 cxd6, play on in a position where it would have been difficult to exploit his two-pawn advantage. There are then opposite-coloured bishops on the board, and the black pieces would be very active. Black's aim is clear—to exchange the knights, after which he will have good

drawing chances. This is precisely why Bondarevsky prefers to decline the Greek gift – the b7 pawn – and retain the knight.

24   ...   ♖f6

The black rook is forced to retreat along the f-file. After 24 ... ♖h4 there follows 25 ♖g8 ♖xh3 26 ♘xc7! ♘xc7 27 d6+ ♔f7 28 dxc7 ♖xg8 and 29 ♖d8 wins.

25   ♗h5!

This move demonstrates White's idea. To deprive his opponent of any drawing chances, which would have been possible with opposite-coloured bishops, he prepares to exchange his bishop for the black knight. If Black tries to avoid the exchange by way of 25 ... ♘d6, there follows 26 c5 ♘b5 27 ♖e1 ♖f5 28 ♗e2 ♖a5 29 ♗g4 with a quick win. So the move 25 ♗h5! forces an exchange profitable for White.

25   ...   c6
26   ♗xe8   ♖xe8
27   ♘c5   cxd5

An attempt to regain a pawn by means of 27 ... ♖ef8 would fail – 28 ♘e4 ♖f4 29 d6+ ♔d8 30 ♖e1!

28   ♖xd5   ♖d8
29   ♖xd8

White does not miss the opportunity to simplify further, nor is he tempted to take the central pawn: 29 ♖xe5+, since after 29 ♔f7, Black's rooks would become active and resistance firm up.

29   ...   ♔xd8
30   ♘xa4   ♖f3
31   ♘c5   ♔c7

32   h4

and White realized his material advantage.

In complex middlegame positions, rich in tactical opportunities, the so called tempo-gaining exchange acquires great potential in the process of realizing a material advantage; with its help one can deprive the opponent of counterplay.

Nesis–Pavlenko
Correspondence 1973/4

60
B

White has the advantage of an extra pawn. However, exploiting the fact that White's knight is undefended, Black makes a central thrust.

29   ...   e5
30   d5   exf4
31   ♘b6

The white knight takes aim at his opponent's bishop and prepares a tempo-gaining rook exchange.

31   ...   ♖a7
32   dxc6!

Forcing a decisive exchange on the d-file. Black cannot save the game with 32 ... ♖xa2 33 ♖xd8! (exchange of the queen for two

rooks is in White's favour) 33 ... ♖xd2 34 ♖xd2 with decisive threats.

32   ...   ♖xd3
33   ♕xd3

This exchange can be described as a tempo-gaining exchange for White, since Black now has to waste a tempo to save his bishop, undefended after the rook exchange; this in turn leads to further material loss.

33   ...   ♗e6
34   cxb7   ♖xb7

Forced, otherwise the white passed pawns are unstoppable.

35   ♗xb7   ♕xb7
36   a4   fxg3
37   hxg3

Black is unable to exploit the weakened position of the white king, since on 37 ... ♗h3 there follows yet another thematic exchange – 38 ♕d5+.

Black resigned after a few moves.

To show the power of consecutively using such a strong and effective weapon as the exchange, we examine the following game in its complete form. In the middlegame Alekhine's position is slightly the more favourable; he then wins a pawn and, finally, with the help of an exchange, realizes his material advantage.

Alekhine–Euwe
World Championship, 24th game
1937

Queen's Gambit

1   ♘f3   d5

2	c4	e6
3	d4	♘f6
4	♘c3	c5
5	cxd5	♘xd5
6	g3	

The move chosen by Alekhine offers his opponent a series of central exchanges and an opportunity to simplify. However, this by no means indicates a desire to draw the game, as is evident from further play.

6	...	cxd4
7	♘xd5	♕xd5
8	♕xd4	♕xd4
9	♘xd4	

61
B

In spite of the queen exchange, the position remains middlegame in character and a quiet endgame is still far away. Kotov, Grandmaster and chess writer, gave a subtle psychological appraisal of the emerging situation: "What is it – a draw? – many a young chessplayer and his friends would ask, losing interest in the game after the exchange of queens. And in many such cases the game does finish in a draw. But here and now various pitfalls are concealed in

the position, as well as innumerable opportunities for the inventive mind ... Yes, it is worthwhile playing on after a queen exchange; there are many finesses in simple positions; there is a wide range of ideas, full of tricky combinative motifs to be explored.

9	...	♗b4+
10	♗d2	♗xd2+
11	♔xd2	♔e7?

In Alekhine's opinion, Black should have played 11 ... ♗d7 to meet the requirements of the position – 12 ♗g2 ♘c6 13 ♘xc6 ♗xc6 14 ♗xc6 bxc6 15 ♖ac1 0-0-0+ 16 ♔e3 ♔c7, with an easy defence in a rook ending.

| 12 | ♗g2 | ♖d8 |
| 13 | ♔e3 | |

The comparative activity of his pieces is clearly in White's favour. He finishes his development easily, while Black's queenside remains frozen. Such an advantage becomes most significant in simple positions.

| 13 | ... | ♘a6 |

This move stops the white rook penetrating to the seventh rank, but the unsatisfactory position of the knight at the edge of the board will cause Black fresh troubles.

14	♖ac1	♖b8
15	a3	♗d7
16	f4	f6
17	♗e4!	

Black intended to drive back the white knight from its dominating central position with e5. Alekhine prevented this pawn advance with his last move, since on 17 ... e5 there follows 18 fxe5 fxe5

19 ♘f3 winning a pawn. White also threatens ♗e4–d3xa6, disrupting his opponent's queenside pawns.

| 17 | ... | ♗e8 |

Now on 18 ♗xh7 there follows 18 ... g6 trapping the bishop.

18 b4!

Playing on both wings, White threatens to win the knight with 19 b5! The unlucky knight on a6 is a source of constant concern to Black.

| 18 | ... | ♖d7 |
| 19 | f5! | ♘c7 |

Black has to give up a pawn. If 19 ... e5, then 20 ♘e6, and Black is helpless.

20	fxe6	♘xe6
21	♘xe6	♔xe6
22	♗xh7	

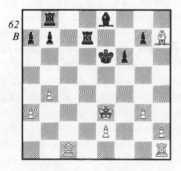

62
B

So White has won a pawn. Let us examine the manner in which Alekhine realizes his advantage. For us it is particularly interesting that by means of an exchange he sets up the optimal dynamic balance for realizing his advantage.

| 22 | ... | f5 |
| 23 | ♖c5! | |

Alekhine, preparing to exchange bishops, chooses further simplifications.

23	...	g6
24	♗g8+	♔f6
25	♖hc1	♖e7+
26	♔f2	♗c6

Black closes the c-file and prevents the intrusion of the white rook on the seventh rank. With his subsequent moves Alekhine forces the bishop exchange, seizing the central white squares.

27	♗d5	♖be8
28	♖e1	♗xd5
29	♖xd5	g5
30	♖d6+	♔e5?

White has the advantage but even now, after the exchange of the bishop, it is not easy to win the game. However, Euwe's last move facilitates White's task. The black king now falls into a mating net. 30 ... ♔f7 would have been more cautious.

The game continued as follows: **31 ♖ed1 g4 32 ♖1d5+ ♔e4 33 ♖d4+ ♔e5 34 ♔e3.** Mate is threatened, so Black is forced to let the enemy king advance. **34 ... ♖e6** (bad is 34 ... f4+ 35 ♔d3 fxg3 36 ♖4d5+ ♔f4 37 ♖f6 mate) **35 ♖4d5+ ♔f6+ 36 ♔f4.**

With the downfall of the f5 and g4 pawns inevitable, the result of the game is obvious. **Black** soon **resigned**.

The games we have examined enable us to draw some conclusions. In the middlegame the principle methods of realizing a material advantage by means of the exchange are as follows: **1.**

Simplifying for a transition into a favourable ending. 2. Translating an excess of material into a decisive positional advantage.

The player with the material deficit is usually faced with an obligatory exchange, or the threat of an exchange compels him to give away fresh material or make positional concessions.

The Exchange in Attack and Defence; the Exchange as an Integral Part of the Combination

The problem of attack and defence appeared simultaneously with the origin of chess, for the constant dynamic between these two things is the quintessence of the game.

The true nature of this creative dynamic has unfolded on the chessboard through the contestants' far-sighted schemes, based on their imagination, their accurate calculations and correct evaluation of each position. With regard to various defensive, and especially attacking operations, a vast body of historical work has been devoted to the strategy and tactics of chess.

Considering the vital rôle and widespread application of the exchange in chess, it is strange that a special study of this most important expedient has virtually never been attempted. Our main interest will be the exchange as a technical tool both in attack and defence, with the aim of creating the optional dynamic balance for resolving a strategic or tactical problem in a given situation.

So, the exchange can be used to eliminate defending pieces with a subsequent mating combination, or as a means of acquiring positional advantage, or to force a transposition into a favourable endgame.

The exchange, also an important expedient to the *defending* player, can be used to reduce an opponent's attacking potential, to create strategically the most favourable conditions in the ensuing struggle.

Since the special character of the subject we are investigating often comes into conflict with a combinative decision – and an investigation of combinations is outside our scope – we shall limit ourselves to interpreting the term combination according to the view of Roklin, the well-known Soviet instructor and methodologist; a view that is invaluable for the practical chessplayer: "A combination is a dynamic variation, made up of forcing moves, usually associated with a sacrifice of material by the attacking side, and finishing with a profitable result." We hasten to make the reservation that we shall be interested only in those combinations where exchanges take place between equivalent pieces, that is, pieces of the same absolute values – otherwise it is not an exchange but a sacrifice – and in combinations in which the exchange is a component. Quite often the exchange comes as a prelude to a complex combinative operation.

So in this chapter we shall familiarize ourselves with two aspects of the exchange:

a. The exchange as part of a combination – tactical exchange – and

b. The exchange in attack and defence, with strategic objectives.

The exchange as part of a combination does not usually have a strategic aim. Its purpose is purely tactical. It can have various motives – to remove defensive pieces, to act as a distraction, or to free files, but the exchange itself must be in the form of a tempo – so that the opponent's reply is more or less obligatory.

Em. Lasker–Maroczy
Paris 1900

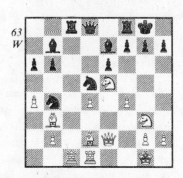

Lasker, well ahead in the development of an initiative, embarks on a crucial operation.

| 20 | f5! | ♖xc1 |
| 21 | ♖xc1 | exf5 |

| 22 | ♘xf5 | ♗f6 |

A tactical mistake, but Black is already in trouble.

| 23 | ♗xb4! |

The exchange is necessary here to free the a2–g8 diagonal. It should be noted that in this case the exchange of the bishop does not diminish White's attacking potential, as the attack is carried out on white squares.

23	...	♘xb4
24	♘xf7	♖xf7
25	♕e6

With this move White's combination is concluded. The black pieces cannot cut off the white bishop: 25 ... ♘d5 26 ♘d6 ♕d7 27 ♕xf7+ ♕xf7 28 ♘xf7 ♔xf7 29 ♖c7+ or 25 ... ♗d5 26 ♗xd5 ♕xd5 (*26 ... ♘xd5 27 ♖c8*) 27 ♖c8+ ♗d8 28 ♘e7+. The game continued: **25 ... ♔h8 26 ♕xf7 ♗xd4+ 27 ♔h1 ♘d3 28 ♖f1 ♗xg2+ 29 ♔xg2 ♕g5+ 30 ♔h3. Black resigned.**

Palmer–Reshevsky
Detroit 1923

White's last move was 21 f4, attacking the knight. However, he did not take into consideration his opponents hidden tactical opportunity.

21   ...   ♛xb2!

This move forces a queen exchange and at the same time begins a subtle positional combination.

22   ♕xb2   ♖xb2
23   fxe5   fxe5+
24   ♔e1   ♖f4!

The black rooks, having acquired great activity, together fall upon the white king.

25   ♘xc4   ♖xa2
26   ♘e3

In spite of his extra piece, White's position is not easy. After 26 ♘d2, play would have continued 26 ... ♖a1+ 27 ♗d1 ♗xg4 28 ♖xg4 ♖xg4, and in the case of 26 ♗d3, strong is 26 ... ♗b5! 27 ♔d1 ♖f3 28 ♗e2 ♖c3!

26   ...   ♖xe4
27   ♖g3   ♖a1+
28   ♗d1

Both of White's minor pieces are unpleasantly pinned and his king cannot find a safe haven.

28   ...   ♗a4
29   ♔e2   ♖a2+
30   ♔e1

In the case of 30 ♔d3, ♖d4+ 31 ♔c3 ♗xd1 32 ♖xd1 ♖xd1 33 ♘xd1 ♖a3+ and White loses a rook.

30   ...   ♗xd1

White resigned.

Lobosh–Janak
Czechoslovakia 1981

We have a complex middle-

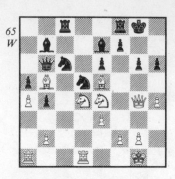

65
W

game position on the board, full of tactical potentiality. Indeed the centre is "a mass of horses and people". The position of the black king gives cause for concern.

White's dark-squared bishop will have an important task in the ensuing play, so White has to retain it, while its light-squared colleague – less valuable – will be exchanged.

1   ♗xc6!   ♗xc6
2   ♘xe6!

Clearly this exchange was the first phase of an interesting forcing operation, demanding accurate evaluation.

2   ...   ♗d7

White must have anticipated this *intermezzo* in good time.

3   ♖xd5   ♗xe6
4   ♕f4!

And this is the tactical basis of White's combinative action! The queen now creates a decisive threat.

4   ...   ♗xd5

4 ... g5 is bad, because of 5 ♘f6+.

5   ♕xh6   f6
6   ♕xg6+   ♔h8
7   ♘g5!

The finale. **Black resigned.**

Particularly interesting are combinative attacks in which exchanges interlace with other tactical devices.

Stein–Osnos
Tallinn 1959

The position is evidently of the Sicilian pattern. Stein, the eminent Soviet Grandmaster, played one of the aggressive variations, constantly hurling his pieces into action.

Black carelessly attacked the white bishop with his last move and an unpleasant surprise waits for him.

14 fxe6!   bxc4

14 ... fxe6 gives White a number of choices, among which the following was well worth consideration: 15 ♘xb5! ♗xb5 (*15 ... ♖b8 16 ♗d2*) 16 ♗xe6+ ♔f8 17 ♗xf6 ♗xf1 18 ♗xg7+ ♔e8 19 ♖xf1 with a winning position.

15 ♖f5

An important intermediate move.

15 ...   ♕b4

16 ♗xf6!

It turns out that White planned for something more than a bishop exchange (16 exd7 ♖ab8! with counterplay). Instead, he exchanges with Black's knight, seizing control of the important d5 square. The exchange was worth the sacrifice!

16 ...   ♗xf6

17 exf7+   ♔f8

The king has no choice of moves.

18 ♖xf6   ♗g4

After 18 ... gxf6 19 ♕xf6 Black would be defenceless against the threat 20 ♕h8+. But now White continues the attack with a material advantage. The outcome of the battle is clear.

19 ♖xd6   ♖db8

20 ♖f1   ♕xb2+

21 ♔d2   ♕b7

22 ♕c5   ♕e7

23 ♘d5   ♕g5+

24 ♖f4!

The white batteries are ready for a final storming. **Black resigned.**

We shall now examine a game that is not without mistakes but is profitably on the same theme.

Psakhis–Mestel
Graz 1981

White sacrificed a pawn in the opening, for which he has acquired strong pressure along the half-open g- and h-files. Black, defending skilfully, has apparently parried the immediate threats.

23 ...   ♘df6

Possibly 23 ... ♘f8 may have

been more accurate, securing control of the e6 square, but the English player has other plans.

24	♘b6	♖b8
25	♘xc8	

Black intended to drive back the menacing knight with 25 ... h6, but the Soviet champion prepares an interesting tactic. At the critical moment he exchanges Black's queen's bishop.

25	...	♕xc8
26	♖ah3	h6

After 26 ... h5 27 ♖g3, White would also have had excellent prospects.

27   ♖xh6!

Black expected only the natural 27 ♘e6+, where after 27 ... ♖xe6! 28 dxe6 ♕xe6! he would have obtained full compensation for giving up the exchange.

27	...	♘xh6
28	♘e6+	♖xe6
29	♕xh6+	♔f7
30	♖g1!	

An interesting situation! The black rook is under attack but cannot move away because of mate in a few moves. An attempt to defend the g6 pawn is also refuted; for instance: 30 ... ♕g8

31 ♖xg6! ♕xg6 32 dxe6+ or 30 ... ♘e8 31 dxe6+ ♕xe6 32 ♖xg6! ♕xg6 33 ♗h5. And yet there is a saving move – 30 ... ♕h8! – 31 ♕xg6+ ♔e7 32 dxe6 (*32 ♕f5 is bad in view of 32 ... ♘xd5!*) 32 ... ♕g8! and White's attack is parried.

30	...	♕f8(?)
31	♕xg6+	♔e7
32	♕f5!	

This manoeuvre results in victory for White.

32   ...   ♘xd5

Black could not save the game with either 32 ... ♕f7 33 dxe6 ♕f8 34 ♖g6 ♕h8 35 ♖xf6! ♕xf6 36 ♕h7+ ♔f8 37 e7+, or 32 ... ♖e8 33 ♖g6 ♔d8 34 dxe6 with a won position for White.

33   ♕h7+

This check would have been impossible with the black queen on h8.

33	...	♔e8
34	♗h5+	

Black resigned

Stein–Tal
Soviet Team Championship
Moscow 1961

The weakness of the black

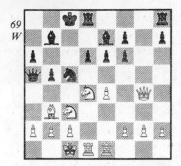

69
W

king's pawn cover gives White an opportunity for direct attack. In the first place, Stein exchanges off his opponent's main defender – the light-squared bishop.

15 ♗d5!

In undertaking this positionally well-justified exchange, it was necessary to consider Black's reply.

15 ... b4
16 ♗xb7+ ♚xb7
17 ♘d5!

A typical thrust in a Sicilian type of formation. Black is forced to immediately accept the sacrifice. He could not avoid it by 17 ... ♗f8 18 ♕h5! exd5 19 ♕xf7+ ♖d7 20 ♕xd5+ with a decisive attack, nor by 17 ... h5 18 ♕g7 exd5 19 exd5 ♖he8 20 ♕xf7 ♕c7 21 ♘c6 ♗f8 22 ♖xe8!

The *intermezzo* 17 ... ♖hg8 would be followed with the effective 18 ♘c6! with an immediate crushing attack.

17 ... exd5
18 exd5 ♖d7
19 ♘c6

This invasion was made possible only as a result of the important exchange on the 16th move.

19 ... ♕xa2!

The passive 19 ... ♕c7 20 ♕xb4+ ♚c8 21 ♕c4! would have given Black little chance of success. In keeping with his style, Tal engages in active counterplay. In the ensuing tactical battle White must strain with all his might to tip the scales in his favour.

20 ♕xb4+ ♚c7
21 ♘xe7 ♖b8
22 ♕a3 ♕c4
23 ♘c6 ♖b3
24 ♕a5+ ♖b6

On 24 ... ♚b7 Black would have lost in view of 25 ♖e8 with unavoidable mate.

25 ♚b1

White is forced to waste a tempo because of the threat of 25 ... ♘b3+

25 ... ♘a4
26 ♖d4 ♘xb2!?

Sharp, but still insufficient.

27 ♚c1!

An excellent move, disentangling the situation at once. 27 ♖xc4? would be a mistake in view of 27 ... ♘xc4+ and Black is out of trouble. But now the unfortunate knight cannot escape from the snare.

27 ... ♕c5
28 ♖e3

With the threat of 29 ♖b3

28 ... ♚b7
29 ♖c3 ♖b5!?

Expecting 30 ♖xc5 dxc5! However, White's cool reply leads to the exchange of queens and the battle is over.

30 ♕a3! ♕xa3
31 ♖xa3 ♖xd5

32   ♘a5+
Black resigned.

An exchange combination can effectively expose a weakness in the opponent's opening configuration.

Uhlmann–Klaric
Sarajevo 1981

70
W

Black played the opening stages of the game carelessly, weakening his kingside pawns for no particular reason; delaying castling. Although Black's dark-squared bishop is awkwardly placed, it could be stabilized by means of a5–a4, followed by castling short, connecting his rooks in readiness for the ensuing struggle. Taking these circumstances into consideration, the German Grandmaster carries out an elegant exchange combination with the object of opening and seizing control of the a-file.

13   b4!   axb4
13 ... ♗a7 was worth considering.

14   axb4   ♖xa1
Black has to concede the open file.

15   ♕xa1   ♘xf3+
Acceptance of the pawn sacrifice would quickly lead to catastrophe: 15 ... ♗xb4 16 ♘xe5 dxe5 17 ♕a8+ ♕d8 18 ♕xd8+ ♔xd8 19 ♗xe5. With the exchange of queens Black is deprived of the defence of the e5 square and the knight on f6. This variation falls precisely within our theme: Black's strategic weaknesses are exposed; his position becomes indefensible. For instance, after 19 ... ♗xc3 20 ♗xc3 ♔e7 21 ♗b4+ ♔e8 22 e5 or 21 ... ♔e6 22 e5! ♔xe5 23 f4+! gxf4 24 ♗c3+ ♔f5 25 ♗d3+ ♔g5 26 h4+. At the same time, his king would be unable to find shelter by castling and his forces would suffer heavy losses.

16   ♗xf3   ♗d4
16 ... ♗xb4 would be bad in view of 17 ♘d5.

17   ♖d1   c5
Exchanging the unlucky bishop could not be achieved with impunity: 17 ... ♗e5 18 ♗xe5 dxe5 19 ♕a8+ ♕d8 20 ♕xb7.

18   bxc5   dxc5
19   e5!
A decisive advance in the centre, after which Black's pieces completely lose any coordination and his position collapses like a pack of cards.

19   ...   ♘g4
Black would not save the game with the other knight move either: 19 ... ♘h7 20 ♕a8+ ♕d8 21 ♕xb7! ♗xc3 22 ♖xd7 ♕xd7 23 ♗c6.

20   ♕a8+   ♕d8

21 ♕xb7 h5

And here on 21 ... ♗xc3 22 ♖xd7! is conclusive.

22 ♘e4!

As before, the e5 pawn cannot be taken: 22 ... ♘xe5 23 ♗xe5 ♗xe5 24 ♘xc5.

22 ... ♖h6

Black tries to finish his development, but now his king is doomed.

23 h3 ♗c6
24 ♘d6+! ♕xd6

On 24 ... ♖xd6 25 ♗xc6+ wins.

25 ♕c8+! ♕d8
26 ♗xc6+ ♔e7
27 ♕b7+ ♔f8
28 ♗d5 ♖e6
29 hxg4

Black resigned.

In the games of the Hungarian Grandmaster Portisch, one of the most outstanding chessplayers of our time, one can find deep strategical ideas and brilliant combinational attacks.

Here is an example from one of Portisch's games which is relevant to our theme.

Portisch–Christiansen
London 1982

White is attacking on the kingside. White's h-pawn plays an important rôle; at an opportune moment it can advance to h6 and immediately the black king's position would be bleak, but only if Black weakens the eighth rank!

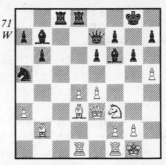

71
W

But the reader may be puzzled – how can one talk about a weakness on the eighth rank with the two black rooks placed on it?

The answer is that they can be exchanged!

19 ♖c1! a6
20 ♖xc8 ♖xc8
21 ♖c1 ♖xc1+
22 ♕xc1 ♕d8

So now the necessary strategic exchanges have been accomplished, the exploitation of the eighth rank can go ahead.

23 h6! ♕c8

It is easy to understand Black's offer of a queen exchange – this would be absolutely in favour of the defending side. But this does not correspond with Portisch's plans!

24 ♕f4! ♕d8
25 ♘e5 b5
26 ♗c3 ♘c4?!
27 ♗xc4 bxc4

There now appears a combinative opportunity for White, deciding the fate of the game. But we must emphasize that the precondition for this opportunity was established on the 19th move, when White undertook the rook exchange.

28   ♗a5!   ♛e7
29   ♘d7!
Black resigned.

If 29 ... ♛xd7 30 ♛xf6 is decisive, and if the black bishop moves away from f6, then 30 ♛b8+ and Black is lost.

The reader's attention has already been drawn to the circumspection required when embarking on exchanges, which give rise to a qualitative transformation on the board. This is particularly important when the opposing forces are in close proximity and the dormant energy of the pieces explodes into life. This sudden change can be quite remarkable.

It is interesting to follow an example in which the exchange takes the form of an intermediate move in a complex combination.

Alekhine–Marshall
Baden–Baden 1925

72
W

22   ♗c4!
This move forces exchanges favourable to White.

22   ...   ♘xc3
23   ♖xd8

The intermediate exchange of rooks enables White to carry out an effective tactical thrust.

23   ...   ♖xd8
24   fxg7!

One idea of this combination is shown in the line: 24 ... ♛e8 25 ♗xf7+! ♚xf7 26 ♖f1+ ♚e6 27 ♖f6+ ♚d5 28 ♖f8, and White wins.

24   ...   ♘xa2+
25   ♚b1!

The natural 25 ♗xa2 would allow 25 ... ♛c5+.

25   ...   ♛e8
26   e6   ♗e4+
27   ♚a1

27 ♖xe4 is also possible – 27 ... ♖d1+ 28 ♚c2 ♛a4+ 29 b3 ♘b4+ 30 ♚xd1

27   ...   f6

Black could not save the game with 27 ... fxe6, in view of 28 ♗xe6+ ♛xe6 29 ♛xd8+ ♚xg7 30 ♛d4+ and 31 ♖xe4 winning.

28   e7+   ♖d5
29   ♛xf6   ♛f7
30   e8(♛)+
Black resigned.

We examine yet another classical example of a combinative attack, in which an important step is exchanging with the opponent's active piece.

R. Byrne–Fischer
New York, 1957

The game has only just emerged from the opening into a complex middlegame. Although White dominates the centre, Black's position is preferable, since his

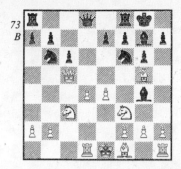

73
B

pieces are better mobilized to take part in the game anywhere on the board. But decisive action is required and the 14-year-old Fischer demonstrates his skill at once.

1 ... ♘a4!

A fine move! This thrust is directed against White's important knight on c3, whose presence upholds the otherwise unstable pawn centre. This move also highlights the exposed position of the unlucky white queen.

2 ♕a3

If White accepts the knight sacrifice, the game could continue with numerous exchanges: 2 ♘xa4 ♘xe4 3 ♗xe7 (*or 3 ♕xe7 ♕a5+ 4 b4 ♕xa4 5 ♕xe4 ♖fe8*) ♘xc5 4 ♗xd8 ♘xa4 5 ♗g5 ♗xf3 6 gxf3 ♘xb2, as a result of which Black would gain an extra pawn and the better position.

2 ... ♘xc3
3 bxc3 ♘xe4
4 ♗xe7 ♕b6!
5 ♗c4

On 5 ♗xf8 Fischer planned the following: 5 ... ♗xf8 6 ♕b3 ♘xc3! 7 ♕xb6 axb6 8 ♖d2 b5 and Black has more than suffi-

cient compensation for the sacrifice of the exchange.

5 ... ♘xc3
6 ♗c5 ♖fe8+
7 ♔f1 ♗e6!

Black continues attacking with enormous energy. If ♗xe6, then a smothered mate follows: 8 ... ♕b5+ 9 ♔g1 ♘e2+ 10 ♔f1 ♘g3+ 11 ♔g1 ♕f1+! 12 ♖xf1 ♘e2 mate!

8 ♗xb6 ♗xc4+
9 ♔g1 ♘e2+
10 ♔f1 ♘xd4+

The mill begins to grind.

11 ♔g1

On 11 ♖d3, 11 ... axb6 12 ♕c3 ♘xf3 13 ♕xc4 ♖e1 mate!

11 ... ♘e2+
12 ♔f1 ♘c3+
13 ♔g1 axb6

Play continued: 14 ♕b4 ♖a4 15 ♕xb6 ♘xd1 and **White resigned.**

Having familiarized ourselves with the rôle of the exchange in preparing tactical operations, we shall now turn our attention to exchanges with longer-lasting, strategic objectives, applied in attack and defence.

Beljavsky–Gufeld
Novosibirsk

We have a familiar pattern on the board. It is clear that the Dragon Variation of the Sicilian Defence has been played against the very sharp Yugoslav Attack. Indeed, using Gufeld's own words, the game is a "battle of missiles and armour plating". The

kings have set up their head-quarters in opposite corners of the battlefield – castling on opposite sides – which guarantees that the impending battle will be sharp in character, with a geometrical increase in the importance of every exchange.

In such middlegame formations the factor determining the outcome of the struggle is not just the seizing of initiative, but also the tempi required to develop the attack. This gives the tempo-gaining exchange an essential rôle.

18   ♘d5!

A typical decision in such positions. White eliminates the enemy monarch's main defence, the f6 knight. It should be noted that this idea is well known; it was applied in a game in 1895 between Marco and Weiss, in which, after 1 e4 c5 2 ♘f3 ♘c6 3 d4 cxd 4 ♘xd4 g6 5 ♘c3 ♗g7 6 ♗e3 d6 7 ♗e2 ♗d7 8 0-0 ♘f6 9 f4 0-0 10 ♕d2 ♖c8 11 h3 a6 12 ♗f3 b5 13 ♘b3 ♕c7 White used the same continuation 14 ♘d5!, but with a somewhat different strategic objective—to open the e-file and exert pressure on the backward e7

pawn. Indeed, after 14 ... ♘xd5 15 exd5 ♘d8 16 c3 ♘b7 17 ♖fe1, White acquired an advantage.

18   ...   ♘xd5

In the light of the above historic example, Black has no alternative. He must exchange the knights, since the pawn thrust on d5 is of a temporary character; moreover the knight was attacking both the queen and the e7 pawn.

19   exd5   ♕b7
20   ♕h2   ♔f7

For the time being the h7 pawn cannot be taken: 21 ♕xh7? ♖h8! trapping the white queen.

21   ♕f4+

With the elimination of the defending knight, the h7 pawn and the whole of Black's kingside are weak. This gives White the opportunity of a quick victory.

21   ...   ♔g8
22   ♖xh7   ♕xd5

After 22 ... ♔xh7? 23 ♕f7! threatening ♖h1 mate.

23   ♖xg7+!

Unfortunately this "Greek" gift cannot be refused.

23   ...   ♔xg7
24   ♘f5+!   ♗xf5
25   ♕h6+   ♔f7
26   ♕xd5

and **Black resigned** within a few moves.

In positions where castling is on the short side, the bishop is often an important defender, particularly when it is fianchettoed. As a rule, forcing the exchange of such a bishop amounts to an achievement for the attacking side.

But sometimes it is useful to exchange with an ordinary bishop if it performs the function of guarding the hostile king.

Kupreichik–Taimanov
44th Soviet Championship

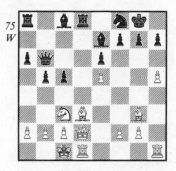

75
W

As in the previous example, castling on opposite sides gives the ensuing struggle a dynamic character. In this type of situation the pieces and pawns of the contestants participate in a race with separate finishing lines. Who can run to the enemy fortifications faster? In the given case White has slightly outstripped his opponent in developing an initiative. However, faced with a counter-attack, "procrastination is like death", so White resorts to a well-tried weapon – a tempo-gaining exchange of an important defender – the e7 bishop.

16   ♗h4!

This move can be regarded as tempo-gaining, because White is not only attacking the undefended bishop; with the help of

the exchange he is also bringing heavy artillery – the h1 rook – into striking position.

16   ...   ♗xh4

Black would not succeed in bringing his queen to defend, since after 16 ... ♕c7? 17 ♗xe7 ♕xe7 18 ♗xh7+ he loses material.

17   ♖xh4   ♗b7
18   ♖g4

What other method except the exchange could have been used to reach such a promising attacking position in two moves?

18   ...   g6
19   ♕g5

This is where Black's exchanged bishop would have been useful: there are no other pieces available to defend the weakened dark squares on the kingside.

19   ...   ♖d7
20   ♖h1   ♕d8

20 ... c4 would have been unsatisfactory in view of 21 ♘e4! For instance, 21 ... cxd3 22 ♘f6+ ♚h8 23 ♘xd7 ♕c7 24 c3 ♕xd7 25 ♕f6+ or 21 ... ♗xe4 22 ♗xe4 ♖ad8 23 ♕f6 ♕d4 24 ♗d3! ♕xg4 25 h6! (Suetin).

21   ♕h6

White's threats intensify with every move, so Black exchanges his rook for the dangerous white bishop.

21   ...   ♖xd3
22   cxd3   ♕xd3
23   ♖f4!

The rook "x-rays" the other defender, the knight at f8. A typical pawn exchange is threatened, opening the f-file to prepare a mating combination: 24 hxg6 fxg6 25 ♖xf8+!

23	...	♛d7
24	♛g5	♛d8

Despite his material deficit Black still hopes for a queen exchange. But Kupreichik, a specialist of the swift attack, is not satisfied merely with the better endgame. He prefers to retain queens and continue storming the king's fortress.

25	♛g4	♛c7
26	♘e4	♗xe4
27	♖xe4	♖d8
28	♖hd1	♖d5
29	♖ee1	c4

It seems that the worst is over for Black. However, the next two exchanges decide the issue.

30	hxg6	hxg6
31	♖xd5!	exd5
32	♛d4	

Despite simplifications, the attack on the dark squares is irresistible.

32	...	♛a5
33	♖h1	♘e6
34	♛h4	♚f8
35	♛f6	

Black resigned.

The following example is an encounter between two of the most outstanding chessplayers of the early seventies, Fischer and Larsen. Their games, always demonstrating important principles, were carried out with great intensity. The creative rivalry of these two players came to a head at the Candidates' Match of 1971, which ended in the sensational result of 6–0 in favour of the American Grandmaster.

Fischer–Larsen
Candidates Match 5th Game
Denver 1971

Black has offered a queen exchange with his last move – 16 ♛c6.

It seems that White, having previously sacrificed a pawn for the initiative, must accept the exchange of his most powerful piece. And yet ...

17   ♖e1!

A magnificent move, which calls to mind Nimzowitsch's proposition: "... The exchange appeared simply as a consequence of occupying strategically important squares."

17   ...   ♛xe4

What did the American Grandmaster intend to play in the case of the preliminary bishop exchange 17 ... ♗xb3? Fischer was prepared only to exchange bishops of the opposite colour. He would have achieved this with the subtle *intermezzo* 18 ♛g4! g6

19 ♖xe7. It is well known that the presence of opposite-coloured bishops favours the attacking side, and here an attempt by Black to exploit a tactical opportunity by means of 19 ... ♗e6 20 ♖xe6 ♕c8 21 ♖e4 f5 would end in catastrophe after 22 ♕h4 fxe4 23 ♕e7!

| 18 | ♖xe4 | d5 |
| 19 | ♖g3 | |

In spite of simplifications, White maintains the pressure as before. Naturally, 19 ... dxe4 is not possible, since after 20 ♖xg7+ White starts up the mill, which is a dangerous adversary for any Don Quixote of the chessboard.

| 19 | ... | g6 |
| 20 | ♗xd5 | ♗d6?! |

We must discuss the reason for this move by the Danish Grandmaster. The point is that the exchange is not just a powerful tactical device but a most important psychological weapon in a sharp struggle. Objectively the strongest continuation would have been the exchange of bishops by means of 20 ... ♗xd5 21 ♖xe7 with the worse but not a desperate position. Being behind in the match by a considerable margin, Larsen was not attracted by such a possibility and tried to complicate the game, but this only increased his difficulties. It is evident that Fischer, the outstanding chessplayer of those days, had allowed for such psychological nuances in the course of the game.

| 21 | ♖xe6! | ♗xg3 |

22	♖e7	♗d6
23	♖xb7	♖ac8
24	c4	a5
25	♖a7	

White has an extra pawn for the exchange, and his two centralized bishops keep the whole board under fire.

25	...	♗c7
26	g3	♖fe8
27	♔f1	♖e7
28	♗f6	♖e3
29	♗c3	h5
30	♖a6!	

With the double threat of 31 ♖c6 and 31 ♖xg6+.

30	...	♗e5
31	♗d2	♖d3
32	♔e2	♖d4
33	♗c3	

Black's attempt to complicate the game has resulted in his having to give back the exchange.

| 33 | ... | ♖cxc4 |

Black could not save the game by transposing into a rook endgame: 33 ... ♖xd5 34 cxd5 ♗xc3 35 bxc3 ♖xc3 36 ♖xa5 ♖c2+ 37 ♔e3 ♖xh2, in view of 38 d6!, and the white pawn cannot be stopped.

34	♗xc4	♖xc4
35	♔d3	♖c5
36	♖xa5	♖xa5
37	♗xa5	♗xb2

Black has restored material equality but to make up for it he has a lost position. The white a-pawn wins the game. Fischer takes the game convincingly to victory: 38 a4 ♔f8 39 ♗c3 ♗xc3 40 ♔xc3 ♔e7 41 ♔d4 ♔d6 42 a5

f6 43 a6 ♔c6 44 a7 ♔b7 45 ♔d5
h4 46 ♔e6 and **Black resigned**.

The threat of exchanging can
be so menacing as to force the
opponent into making some sort
of concession.

Spassky–Petrosian
World Championship Moscow
1969

21   e5

With this move White makes
the e4 square available for his
knight.

21   ...   dxe5
22   ♘e4!

Black's principal defending
pieces are the f6 knight and the f8
bishop and White's move is directed towards their removal.

On 22 ... ♘xe4? there follows
23 ♖xf8 +.

22   ...   ♘h5

The black knight, avoiding the
exchange to defend the g7 square,
must be placed at the edge of the
board.

23   ♕g6

The white pieces have taken up
menacing positions close to the
enemy king.

23   ...   exd4

After 23 ... ♘f4 24 ♖xf4 exf4
25 ♘f3 ♕b6 26 ♖g5! and if 26 ...
hxg5 there follows 27 ♘exg5 and
mate.

24   ♘g5!

If 24 ... hxg5, then 25 ♕xh5 +
♔g8 26 ♕f7 + ♔h8 27 ♖f3 g4
and 28 ♖xg4 wins, so **Black
resigned**.

Within Karpov's arsenal of
outstanding techniques, the
exchange stands as a universal
weapon, enabling him to give the
game the required direction.

Tatai–Karpov
Las Palmas 1977

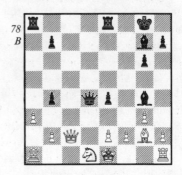

The then World Champion has
obtained a menacing initiative
from a pawn sacrifice. With his
last move 23 ♕c2 White has protected the e2 pawn and neutra-
lized the threat 23 ... ♗f3. The
game has reached a crucial stage.
The outcome now depends largely
on the correct choice of a plan,

and, naturally, its accurate execution. Throughout the history of chess, the ability to seize such critical moments in the course of the game and to concentrate forces to the maximum in precisely these extreme situations– this has always been the hallmark of the highest class of chessplayer.

23 ... ♕d3!

"Fine", the reader might say, "Black exchanges his opponent's only active piece". Just as the tip of the iceberg is clearly visible to everyone, but its true size is known only to the specialist, the effective 23 ... ♕d3! requires deep and accurate evaluation.

24 exd3

If 24 ♘e3, then 24 ... ♕xc2 25 ♘xc2 ♗xb2 and White is lost. Again, Black retains his advantage on 24 ♕d2 ♕xd2+ 25 ♔xd2 ♖ad8+ 26 ♔e1 ♖c8.

24 ... exd3+

25 ♔d2 ♖e2+

26 ♔xd3 ♖d8+

All the black pieces are in play.

27 ♔c4

On 27 ♗d5?! there would follow 27 ... ♖xd5+ 28 ♔c4 ♖xc2+ 29 ♔xd5 ♗f3+! and Black would remain with an extra piece.

27 ... ♖xc2+

28 ♔xb4 ♖cd2!

White's king is under constant fire from the enemy pieces and his own forces can only watch helplessly the downfall of their monarch.

29 f3 ♗f8+

30 ♔a5 ♗d7!

Now White has to defend the g2 bishop, after which 31 ... ♗c5 and 32 ... ♖a8 mate. **White resigned**.

Fischer–Bolbochan
Stockholm 1962

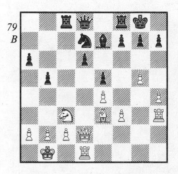

79
B

18 ... ♘b6

19 ♗xb6!

The exchange eliminates the defender of the important d5 square, but how does it fit into our theme of "the exchange in attack"? The black knight is on the queen's flank, while the object of the attack – the black king – is on the opposite side of the board. The answer will become clear in White's subsequent moves.

19 ... ♕xb6

20 ♘d5

The exchange has secured a dominating position for the white knight in the centre. This indestructible knight will play the lead in a direct attack against the enemy king. So, the exchange of the bishop for the black knight has a clear strategic objective – the organization of a kingside attack. It is interesting that Fischer in his book "My 60 Memorable Games" considers this position as already in White's favour.

| 20 | ... | ♛d8 |
| 21 | f4 | |

Threatening 22 f5 and a direct storming of the black king's bastions. Naturally, 21 ♘xe7+ ♛xe7 22 ♛xd6?? is not possible, in view of 22 ... ♖fd8! and Black unexpectedly wins.

21	...	exf4
22	♛xf4	♛d7
23	♛f5!	

An interesting tactical move. As a rule, an attack on a piece of equal value is an offer of an exchange, but in this case Black would lose a piece: 23 ... ♛xf5? 24 ♘xe7+.

23	...	♖cd8
24	♖a3	♛a7
25	♖c3	

An interesting psychological moment. The natural continuation in such situations would be 25 ♘xe7+ ♛xe7 26 ♖xa6 ♖fe8 27 a4!, translating the positional advantage, of the good knight against bad bishop, into a material advantage. However, Fischer prefers to preserve his centralized knight and use it in a conclusive attack.

It should be noted that the more impressive way of exchanging the knight: 25 ♘f6+ ♗xf6 (*bad is 25 ... gxf6 26 gxf6 ♔h8 27 ♛g5 ♖g8 28 fxe7!*) 26 gxf6 g6 27 ♛g5 ♔h8 would not lead to the desired objective.

| 25 | ... | g6! |

An essential *intermezzo*. The immediate 25 ... ♛d7? would lose at once because of 26 ♖c7.

26	♛g4	♛d7
27	♛f3	♛e6
28	♖c7	♖de8

Virtually the only move, since after 28 ... ♖fe8 20 ♖f1 Black is completely helpless.

29	♘f4	♛e5
30	♖d5	♛h8
31	a3	

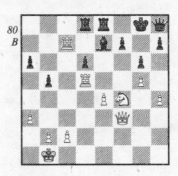

A picturesque position! White has an overwhelming positional advantage. His pieces dominate the board, while the black pieces, deprived of any activity, suffocate on the eighth rank.

| 31 | ... | h6 |
| 32 | gxh6 | ♛xh6 |

In the line shown by Fischer 32 ... ♗xh4 33 ♘xg6! fxg6 34 ♛b3 ♖f7 35 ♖f5, the white knight would have given its life dearly.

| 33 | h5 | ♗g5 |
| 34 | hxg6 | fxg6 |

Again, in the line 34 ... ♗xf4 35 gxf7+ ♖xf7 36 ♖xf7 ♔xf7 37 ♖h5! the knight's life would be very costly.

| 35 | ♛b3! | |

An ambush from which there is no defence.

35	...	♖xf4
36	♖e5+	♔f8
37	♖xe8+	

Black resigned.

In a situation where the attacking side is deficient in material, it is particularly risky to go for an exchange when proceeding with aggressive operations. Having sacrificed a pawn or even a piece, it is very hard to commit oneself to simplifications, since the significance of the material disparity will be enhanced with the further elimination of fighting units from the board. Nevertheless, a well-founded and correctly set-up exchange, even under these conditions, can lead to success. This theme is illustrated in a fine example below, taken from an interesting, creative game of the future world champion, Gary Kasparov, in which he uses Botvinnik's system in the Slav Defence, playing against his future second, Grandmaster Dorfman.

Kasparov–Dorfman
Frunze 1981
49th Soviet Championship

30	...	♗e5

On the day before the above game, Kasparov, playing White against Timoshenko, came to the same position and won quite convincingly after 30 ... e5. Again, the young Grandmaster plays sacrificially. Dorfman picks up the gauntlet and virtually forces a

rook exchange.

31	♖c5	♖xc5
32	♗xc5!	

A brilliant move, not anticipated by Black in his home preparations. Dorfman expected only the natural line 32 ♕xc5 ♘c6 33 ♖b7+ ♗c7! 34 ♗b6 ♖c8, in which case Black gradually repels the attack, retaining his extra piece. But Kasparov's game is not stereotyped: He goes for an exchange which is profitable for himself and carries through his attack successfully. In the absence of his rook shield, the black king is defenceless against threats along the d-file.

32	...	♘c6

On 32 ... ♗c7, 33 ♕d3+ ♔c8 34 ♖b4! is decisive.

33	♕d3+	♔c8

After 33 ... ♘d4 34 ♖d1 the knight falls into a deadly pin, and an attempt to counterattack could be easily parried: 34 ... ♕h3 35 ♗xd4 ♕xh2+ 36 ♔f1 ♕h1+ 37 ♔e2 ♕h5+ 38 f3.

34	♖d1	

The attack on the d-file is a consequence of the rook exchange; Black cannot regain the file with 34 ... ♖d8, in view of 35

♕a6+.

	34	...	♘b8
	35	♖c1!	

Kasparov does not give his opponent a minute's respite. Every one of his moves is like a sharp uppercut.

	35	...	♕a4
	36	♗d6+	♘c6
	37	♗xe5	♖d8
	38	♕b1!	

White forces his way through the b-file and at the same time prevents the exchange of rooks on d1.

	38	...	♖d5
	39	♕b8+	♔d7
	40	♕c7+	♔e8

And now the familiar exchange combination, leading to an easily won rook ending.

	41	♕xc6+	♕xc6
	42	♖xc6	♖xe5
	43	♖c8+	

Black resigned.

In the middlegame the defending side is faced with a whole series of complex problems. It could be a question of repelling a direct attack, or neutralizing positional pressure, or the possibility of counterattacking if the opponent goes too far with his offensive.

The exchange is one of the most effective means of resolving all these problems.

Let us examine a simple example.

Seirawan–Hort
Bad–Kissingen 1981

In spite of the absence of

queens the strategic outline of the struggle is still middlegame in character. The white knight is attacking two pieces and the position of the black king looks insecure. Black is in a critical situation, but the resourceful defender finds an excellent countermove:

	34	...	♗g5!

With the help of an ingenous tactical trick, Black forces the exchange of the dangerous knight, and chances for the two sides are equalized.

| | 35 | ♗xg5 | |

The attempt to win a pawn in the line: 35 ♘xe8 ♗xh6 36 ♘d6 ♗xe3 37 ♘xf7+ ♔g8 38 ♘d6 ♘d4 39 ♘xb7 f4! would be risky, with the black minor pieces ideally placed to cut off the white king from the passed f-pawn.

	35	...	♔xg7
	36	♖c3	

Already White has to play with precision.

	36	...	♘d4
	37	♔c1	♗g6
	38	♗e3	♖d8
	39	a4	

And in this position of approximate dynamic equality, a **draw** was **agreed**.

As in attack, so in defence, one must pay close attention to the exchange, with due consideration for the character of the position arising.

As a rule, the chances of success for the attacking side will recede with the exchange of a piece, while the defender's possibilities will increase.

Simagin–Smyslov
Moscow 1959

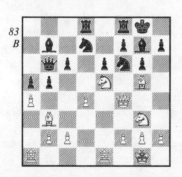

83
B

15 ...   ♘xe5!

This exchange demanded from Smyslov an accurate appraisal of the emerging position and evaluations of intricate variations.

16   ♗xf6

If 16 dxe5, then 16 ... ♖d4! 17 ♕e3 ♘g4, and Black gains the initiative.

16 ...   ♗xf6

17   ♕xf6

Although two pairs of minor pieces have been eliminated from the board and there has been a qualitative change in the situation, it seems that Black has not

improved his position: the white queen is entrenched on f6; the black knight has to cover e6 from the rook's attack.

But ...

17 ...   ♘g4!

Black attacks the queen; play proceeds with gain of tempo.

18   ♕f4   ♖xd4

19   ♖e4   ♖xe4

20   ♘xe4   c5!

This move must have been foreseen. Now White must find resourceful play just to maintain equality.

21   ♕xg4   f5

22   ♘f6+   ♖xf6

23   ♕g5   ♔g7

24   axb5   ♕xb5

25   ♕f4

After these sharp tactical skirmishes, let us evaluate the position. White has the initiative for the loss of a pawn; however, it should be noted that with the help of the exchanges Smyslov has managed to make his position safe, and the worst is over for Black. Consequently, after a few moves the game ended in a **draw**.

We offer the reader a fragment from a game between Polugayevsky and Karpov, in which the exchange was of an auxiliary character but resolved defensive problems.

Polugayevsky–Karpov
Moscow 1974

As a result of Black's last move 40 ... ♘f5–d6!, Polygayevsky is with a critical position: his queen

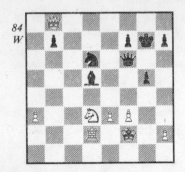

is out of play at b8; he must also parry the threats of 41 ... ♕xf3 + and 41 ... ♘e4 + .

41   ♘f4!

With one move White has resolved all his problems!

In the same instant he has closed the f-file, along which Black directed his main thrust, and opened the d-file for his rook, as well as threatening 42 ♘h5 + .

41   ...   gxf4
42   ♖xd5

The above play is of direct relevance to our theme.

By means of a tactical expedient White has swapped off the strong black bishop at d5. That is fine, but further play is not so simple, and the subsequent battle required an accurate appraisal by White.

42   ...   ♕b2 +

On 42 ... fxe3 + , Polugayevsky intended 43 ♔xe3 ♕e6 + 44 ♔d4 with a forced draw.

43   ♔f1!

Not 43 ♔g1? ♕b1 + and 44 ... ♕a2 + winning the rook.

In this position a **draw** was **agreed** in view of the line 43 ... fxe3 44 ♖g5 + ♔h6 45 ♕xd6 +

♔xg5 46 ♕e7 + ♔f4 47 ♕e4 + and 48 ♕xe3.

An experienced player, forced into defence, always looks for counterattacking opportunities, well aware that passive defence harbours the germ of defeat. All chessplayers aspiring to reach a high level must be able to defend– it is so much more difficult to press home a swift attack against a skilfully defending opponent. In modern chess one must possess a whole arsenal of resources in order to have a chance of success.

We quote the following remarks regarding the problems of defence by Polugayevsky the well-known specialist of the counter-attack:

"Defence is a superb arena for developing the character – as a chessplayer and a human being. The rôle of the defender is complex and responsible. A wise attacking player will always have some means of withdrawing from his attack and transposing play into an acceptable endgame etc."

"In defence it is sometimes necessary to find a series of crucial moves, with no alternatives, in order to hold the position. . . . . . On the other hand, one can learn a great deal from defence:- above all, from active defence! The ability to wait for an opportune moment for the counterthrust, to find counterplay on the opposite wing, to sacrifice a pawn, the exchange or even the queen, in order to change the character of the battle and go over into the attack. It seems to me that it is not accidental that World Champions, in addition to other qualities, were all superb masters of defence."

Portisch–Polugayevsky
Budapest 1963

85
B

21 ...   ♘b2!

Black would be prepared, even at the cost of a pawn, to exchange his knight for his opponent's strong bishop, in which case he would have the bishop pair and pressure along the a-file. A typical example of active defence!

22 ♔h1   ♗xc5!

It is essential to exchange the dangerous knight.

23 bxc5

In the case of 23 ♘xc5 b6 24 ♘b3 ♗a6, Black has an excellent game.

23 ...   ♕d3

Black intercepts White's initiative. On 24 ♕xd3 ♘xd3 25 ♖e3 ♘b2, Black threatens with the unpleasant 26 ... ♘d5.

24	♖f2	♘g4
25	♖d2	♕xc2
26	♖xc2	♘d3

| 27 | ♖ee2 | ♗e6 |

After the exchange of queens, the black minor pieces acquire great activity.

28 ♘a5

White has decided to give up a pawn. Polugayevsky recommends 28 ♘d4! ♗c4 29 h3 ♘f6 30 ♘f5! ♘xc5 31 ♘xg7! ♗xe2 32 ♘xe8 ♖xe8 33 ♗xf6 ♘xe4 34 ♗xe4 ♖xe4 35 ♖c3 with drawing chances.

28	...	♘xc5
29	h3	♘f6
30	♗xf6	♖xa5
31	♗d4	♘a6
32	f5	♖a4!

It is interesting that for every one of White's blows Black answers with a counter thrust. The Exchange of opposite-coloured bishops will increase Black's chances.

33	fxe6	♖xd4
34	exf7+	♔xf7
35	♖c3	♖ed8
36	♖xa3	♖d3

As a result of the multiple exchanges the position has simplified. The black pieces are now slightly more active.

37	♖xd3	♖xd3
38	♔h2	♔e6
39	e5	♖a3
40	♗e4	g6
41	♗c2	♘c5
42	♔g2	♔e7!

Forcing the white bishop to take up an unsatisfactory position.

43	♗d1	♘d3
44	♗b3	♘c1
45	♖e3	h6

Black has a won position. The game continued as follows: **46 h4 ♞xb3 47 axb3 ♚e6 48 ♚f3 ♜a5 ♚f4 ♜b5 50 ♜e4 c5 51 ♜e3 ♜b4+ 52 ♚f3 ♜d4 53 g4 g5 and White resigned.**

So, the player *attacking* in the middlegame strives, with the help or the threat of exchanges, to fulfil the following objectives:

1. To acquire a decisive material advantage

2. To force the position into a technically favourable endgame

3. To acquire a decisive positional advantage, thereby forcing the opponent, in parrying various threats, to exchange his own active pieces.

The *defending* side can, with the help of exchanges, **1. Reduce the attacking potential of his opponent, 2. Neutralize his opponent's active play with an organized counterattack, 3. Transpose the game into a technically drawn ending or create a dynamic balance with characteristically drawish tendencies.**

Realizing a Positional Advantage

There are many authoritative works devoted to the study of positional play, including analysis of numerous games in which the positional motif is prominent. However, the exchange as an expedient in the strategic struggle has received little attention. We shall be interested in the manner in which the exchange helps to accomplish some positional objective when it is organically

linked with a general strategic plan.

In studying the problems of positional play, it is impossible to leave out the rôle of the plan. We quote Kotov's definition: "A single plan in a game of chess is a totality of consecutive strategic operations, each one of which fulfils, independently, a strategic aim, as dictated by the position arising on the chessboard."

The exchange is such an operation. It can help to open or close files, seize strategically important points, or reveal defects in the disposition of the opponent's pieces.

In the previous chapter we saw excerpts from games in which the exchange was undertaken in order to open files in an attack against the king. In a purely positional game the opening of a file with the aid of an exchange is also widely applied.

Mestel–Karlsson
Las Palmas 1982

86
W

14   ♞b5!

White forces an exchange with a very active and well-placed hostile piece. This subtle exchange is the beginning of a larger strategical plan, the objective being the opening of the c-file and its seizure by the heavy pieces. Furthermore, after the exchange of knights, the dominating c4 will be available for the white bishop.

14 ...   ♘xb5

A forced reply in view of the weakness of the d6 pawn.

15   cxb5   ♛c7+

We should point out that White forced the knight exchange in conjunction with an intended pawn sacrifice. However, Karlsson, preferring safe play, refuses the f-pawn. Indeed, taking it would have placed Black in a particularly dangerous predicament in view of the white bishop entering into the fray against the precariously situated black king. For instance, 15 ... gxf5 16 ♗c4+ ♚f8 17 ♖hf1 f4 18 ♛h4 h5 19 g3 ♗g4 20 gxf4 ♗xd1 21 fxe5 ♖h6 22 ♛g5 with decisive threats.

16   ♚b1   ♗d7

And now 16 ... gxf5 17 ♖c1 followed by 18 ♗c4+ would have given White a very strong attack.

17   b3   ♖ad8

18   ♗c4+

One of the aims of the exchange has been fulfilled. In place of the pawn the long-range bishop occupies c4.

18   ...   ♚g7

19   h4   ♗e8

20   h5   g5

21   h6+   ♚f8

22   ♛d3

The young English Grandmaster shows outstanding strategic skill. Firstly, he constricts his opponent on the kingside and shuts the black rook out of the game. And then, with his dynamic advantage in strength, he accomplishes the main task of the general plan – the seizure of the open c-file which will be used for a conclusive invasion with his heavy artillery.

22   ...   ♛c5

23   a4   a6

24   bxa6   bxa6

25   ♖c1!

Securing an invasion on the open file.

25   ...   ♖b8

26   ♚a2   ♚e7

27   ♗e6!

The bishop, taking up with gain of tempo position on the key e6 square, breaks up completely the coordination of the hostile forces.

27   ...   ♛b6

28   ♛c4

The second task of the strategical plan has been fulfilled. The seizure of the c-file is complete; the way into the opponent's camp is open.

28   ...   ♖b7

29   g4   a5

30   ♖hd1   ♖f8

31   ♖d2   ♛b4

32   ♛xb4

White does not avoid the endgame; the complete disharmony of the black pieces will hasten the end all the more.

32	...	axb4
33	♖dc2	♗d7
34	♖c7	

Having exchanged his only active piece, the queen, Black somehow tries to cover the queenside, but White soon wins convincingly.

34	...	♖xc7
35	♖xc7	♖d8
36	a5	♔e8
37	a6	

and **White won**.

We shall now examine a more complex example in which exchange, closely intertwined with the general strategic plan, is associated in particular with the seizure of an open file.

Simagin–Kotov
Moscow 1944

87
W

The game has only just emerged from the opening stages, and Black decides to resolve the development of his queen's bishop by means of the usual pawn advance e6–e5. However, White has an advantage in development, and his light-squared bishop is in a better position than its opposite number in complex variations of the Queen's Gambit. The sum of these advantages gives White an opportunity to undertake the plan of opening a central file.

11	♗g5!

The exchange of his superfluous piece is the first link of White's plan.

11	...	h6
12	♗xf6	♘xf6

12 ... ♕xf6 13 ♘e4 would give White additional opportunities.

13	dxe5	♗xe5
14	♘xe5	♕xe5
15	♕d4	

All logical: the black minor pieces do not have many prospects, and White hastens to take control of the d-file. And yet Black could still carry on in an inferior endgame after 15 ... ♕xd4 16 ♖xd4 ♗e6. Avoiding the queen exchange, Black hopes to obtain counterplay, but it is easier now for White to generate activity.

15	...	♕h5
16	f3	♗h3

An instructive moment. Black should try and retain his bishop and exchange his knight. This could have been achieved by 16 ... ♗e6 with the idea of ... ♘d5, and if 17 e4, then with 17 ... ♕a5!, and 18 ... ♖fd8! Black would have intercepted the d-file.

Had Black taken the above course, the key to appraising the comparative strengths of the minor pieces would have been as follows: the black bishop at e6 protects the d7 intrusion point, and to a certain extent exerts pressure on White's queen's flank, whilst the white king's bishop does not take part in play for the time being; on the other hand, the white knight is considerably more mobile than the black knight. It may seem that this appraisal is rather general, somewhat remote from the actual situation, but it is precisely Black's mistaken view of the comparative potential of the pieces – and in consequence the incorrect evaluation of the exchange offer – that will be Black's downfall.

17	e4	♗xg2
18	♔xg2	♖fe8
19	♖d2	♕a5
20	♖ad1	

White has parried the threat 20 ... ♖ad8 and established full control of the open file. His next task is to further constrain his opponent by means of a pawn advance.

20	...	♖e7
21	♕c4	♖ae8
22	♖d6	♕b6
23	b4	♖e6
24	♖6d4!	

The young Vladimir Simagin shows an astonishingly mature understanding of the position – both rooks are needed in the attack!

24	...	♖6e7
25	♘a4	♕c7
26	♘c5	♕c8
27	♖1d2	♘h7

The apparent attempt to move the black knight to g5 is only a gesture, with considerably more modest intentions.

| 28 | h4 | ♘f8 |
| 29 | ♖d6 | ♘e6?! |

Black commits yet another inaccuracy in his decision regarding the problem of simplification. Although the ending with heavy pieces will be unfavourable to Black, there are no immediate threats against him. 29 ... a6 should have been considered.

| 30 | ♘xe6 | ♖xe6 |

The alternative 30 ... fxe6 – a difficult choice – would have been the lesser evil.

| 31 | ♖xe6 | ♖xe6 |
| 32 | ♕d4! | |

A tactical punishment for a positional imperfection. The double threat of 33 ♕xa7 or ♕d8+ ♕xd8 34 ♖xd8+ ♔h7 35 ♖d7 causes Black to go into a confused defence.

32	...	♕f8
33	f4	♖e8
34	e5	♕e7
35	a3	a6
36	h5!	♕e6
37	♕d7	♖e7 (89)
38	♕xe6!	

Simagin, having fixed his opponent's pawns, acquires an over-

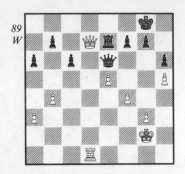

whelming advantage and finds the simplest way to realize it. The whole game, from beginning to end, is very impressive.

38	...	fxe6
39	♔f3	♖c7
40	♔e4	♔f7
41	♖d6	♔e7
42	f5!	

Just in time! The strengthening of the white king's position neutralizes Black's subsequent activity. The rook endgame is a win for White and, in annotating to the finish, we would like to point out the outstanding technique displayed by White throughout the game. **42 ... exf5+ 43 ♔xf5 c5 44 bxc5 ♖xc5 45 ♖b6 ♖c7 46 g4 ♔f7 47 a4 ♔e7 48 a5 ♔f7 49 ♔e4! ♔e7 50 ♔d5 ♖d7+ 51 ♖d6 ♖c7 52 e6 ♔e8 53 ♖b6 ♔e7 54 ♖b1 ♔e8 55 ♖b4 ♖c1** (55 ... ♔e7 56 ♖b6 ♔e8 57 ♔d6 ♖e7 58 ♖b1 ♔d8 59 ♖f1 and White wins) **59 ♖xb7 ♖d1+ 57 ♔e5 ♖e1+ 58 ♔f5 ♖f1+ 59 ♔g6 ♖f4 60 g5 ♖g4 61 ♔xg7 ♖xg5+ 62 ♔f6 Black resigned.**

Seizing open files with the help of the exchange has a special significance when the opponent is behind in development. In these cases positional motifs are closely interlaced with an attack against the king.

Portisch–Hübner
Montreal 1979

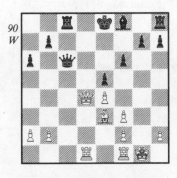

The black king is stuck fast in the centre, but this position is dynamic in character. Were Black given a chance to bring out his bishop and castle, he would have no problems whatsoever. Accurate and resolute action is required from White.

16	♕a7!

Portisch attacks, digging himself into his opponent's camp with the queen, taking aim at the enemy pawns and preparing to exchange Black's active c8 rook.

16	...	♗e7
17	♖c1	♕d7
18	♖xc8+	♕xc8
19	♖c1	

White has exchanged his opponent's active rook and seized control of the open c-file.

19	...	♕d7
20	♕a8+!	

Just so! In the case of the natural 20 ♕b8+ ♗d8 21 ♖c8 ♔e7 22 ♗c5+ ♔e6 23 ♗b6? ♗c7! Black wins!

20	...	♗d8
21	♖c8	♔f7
22	♗b6!	♗xb6
23	♖xh8	♔g6

91 B

White was threatening 24 ♕g8+, while on 23 ... ♗xf2+ the simple 24 ♔g2! would be decisive.

24 ♕e8+

Destroying his opponent's last illusions. After the exchange of queens, White's advantage of rook against bishop becomes overwhelming. **Black resigned** soon afterwards.

In a positional battle, any weakening of the opponent's position is of great significance, particularly creating weak points and deforming his pawn structure.

The exploitation of such weaknesses is an effective way of realizing the positional advantage. In such cases the exchange can be used in two ways. Firstly, the exchange can immediately expose a weak square or pawn; secondly, exchanging with a piece defending the weak point enables one to exploit this defect in the subsequent struggle.

Makagonov–Botvinnik
Sverdlovsk 1945

White has an appreciable defect in his position – the weakness of

the white squares on the kingside. To take advantage of this Black must exchange the light-squared bishops.

13 ... ♗xc3!

Beginning the elimination of the defenders of the e4 square.

14 bxc3 ♗f5!

And now it's the light-squared bishop's turn.

15	♗xf5	♕xf5
16	g4!	

Botvinnik commented: "A splendid move, after which the weakness of the white squares becomes less appreciable."

Now, however, Black exploits another positional factor – the dicey position of the white king.

16	...	♕e6
17	♗a3	♘e4+
18	♔f3	h5
19	h3	f6!

White is faced with a difficult dilemma: to take the f6 pawn, completely weakening his own king's position, or to give up a pawn. He prefers the second option, but this only drags out the struggle: **20 c4 hxg4+ 21 hxg4 ♖xh1 22 ♕xh1 0-0-0 23 ♖d1 fxe5 24 cxd5 cxd5 25 ♖c1+ ♔b8**, and

Black realized his advantage in the ending.

Balashov–Larsen
Buenos Aires 1980

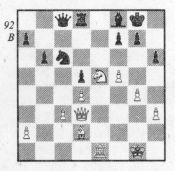

92
B

At first glance the position appears approximately equal. White's chances are in the centre and on the kingside. However, a deeper analysis of the situation indicates serious flaws in White's pawn structure. Exploiting the weakness of the a2 and c3 pawns can be achieved only by simplifying.

31   ...   ♞xe5
32   dxe5

White should have considered 32 ♖xe5 ♗d6 33 ♖e2 and 34 ♕f3. Now the Danish Grandmaster forces a queen exchange, after which White's pawn defects become of greater consequence.

32   ...   ♕c4!
33   ♕xc4

The exchange cannot be avoided, since after 33 ♕f3 d4! the white king is suddenly under attack.

33   ...   dxc4

What a change in the position after the last moves! With the help of the queen exchange, Black has not only created a solid pawn chain, getting rid of his isolated pawn, but also seized the open file with the gain of a tempo.

34   ♖e2   b5
35   ♗e3   ♖d3

The black rook has moved into an ideal position. It controls the d-file, at the same time attacking the pawns on both flanks. White cannot hold on to the c3 pawn, since on 36 ♗d4 there follows 36 ... b4!

36   ♗xa7   ♖xc3
37   ♔g2   ♖d3
38   ♗e3   b4

The black pawns on the queenside are clearly more dangerous than the white pawns on the kingside.

39   h4   b3
40   axb3   cxb3
41   ♗c1   ♗b4
42   ♗b2   ♔f8
43   g5

Now the black king can easily deal with the white pawns. More precise would have been 43 h5.

43   ...   hxg5
44   hxg5   ♗c5
45   e6   fxe6
46   fxe6   ♗d4!

A typical procedure. Black is trying to exchange the blockading pieces. After 47 ♗xd4 ♖xd4 48 ♖b2 ♖b4, with the white king cut off from his pawns, the rook endgame would easily be won by Black. Now the blockade of the black passed pawn is lifted.

47	♗a3+	♚e8
48	g6	♗f6
49	♖f2	♖d5

Black is on the alert. There was a threat of 50 ♖xf6 gxf6 51 g7. After the text move the threat is removed in view of 51 ... ♖g5+.

50 ♔h3

If 50 ♖f3, then 50 ... b2 51 ♖b3 ♖d2+ 52 ♔f3 ♖d3+!

50 ... ♖a5

White resigned.

The exchange plays an important rôle in the occupation of key squares within the opponent's camp. Sometimes just one weak square can cause the loss of the game.

As a rule, the exploitation of weak squares – for example, due to the disposition of the opponent's pieces – is made more difficult by the presence of hostile pieces controlling them. In the battle for the key squares, exchanging with these defenders is of great consequence. We have already met with this motif in the game between Makagonov and Botvinnik. Botvinnik's games are generally rich in material illustrating the use of the exchange in positional battles (93).

Botvinnik–Kan
Leningrad 1939

We show a fragment of a game illustrating the rôle and aim of exchanges in setting up strongholds in the centre.

White's strategic plan, which Botvinnik accomplishes with

93
W

relentless consistency, includes the occupation of the weak d5 square with his bishop.

11	dxe5	dxe5
12	♗d3	h6
13	0-0	0-0
14	f4	♘d7
15	f5!	

Now the e6 square is inaccessible to Black.

| 15 | ... | ♘f6 |

In his comments on the game, Botvinnik criticizes this move on the grounds that "now White receives the opportunity of exchanging knights, after which the bishop in the centre will be complete master."

16	♘e4!	♕d8
17	♘xf6+	♕xf6

With this knight exchange, White has removed the piece guarding the d5 square.

18	♗e4	♖b8
19	♖ad1	b6
20	h3	♗a6
21	♗d5	

The objective has been achieved – the white bishop occupies the dominating square.

21	...	b5
22	cxb5	♖xb5

22 ... ♗xb5 was essential: 23 c4 ♗c6! Although White would have won a pawn in this case after 24 ♕e4 ♗xd5 25 ♖xd5, in Botvinnik's opinion after the exchange of bishops Black would have obtained counterplay along the open b-file.

    23   c4   **♖b6**
    24   ♖b1!
Preventing 24 ... ♗b7.
    24   ...   **♖d8**
    25   ♖xb6   **axb6**
    26   e4

White's bishop is now quite safe on the strong point. White's subsequent attack was based on the great activity of this piece. Soon White won a pawn, and then the game.

Keres–Danielson
Tallinn 1935

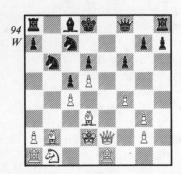

94
W

As a result of an unusual opening strategy, White managed to create a vulnerable point e6 within his opponent's camp. It could be tempting to burst in and occupy this square with the heavy artillery – queen or rook – but for the moment it is safely guarded by two black pieces – the knight and the bishop. The only way of seizing this key point is to exchange with these defenders. To carry out this plan, White must possess squares via which his minor pieces can sneak up on their black colleagues. The most suitable squares for this purpose are the b5 and f5. It is instructive to follow the consistency with which the youthful Keres carried out the intended strategic plan.

    18   ♘c3   **♗d7**
    19   g4   **♔c8**
    20   a4

Black is forced by the threat 21 a5 to automatically stop any further advance of the a-pawn. But this results in White's full control of the b5 square.

    20   ...   **a5**
    21   ♗f5!

Using the f5 square as a springboard, White induces the exchange of the first defender of the key point e6 – the bishop.

    21   ...   **♗xf5**
    22   gxf5   **♕d8**
    23   ♕d3   **♕d7**

The e6 square is a breach in the wall of the black fortress, with the white troops poised to dash through it. Exploiting the fact that, after the exchange of bishops, this square is already controlled by the two pawns, White is now prepared to respond to 23 ... ♖e8 with 24 ♖e6! offering the sacrifice of the exchange: 24 ... ♘xe6 25 fxe6, after which the black pieces, deprived of the

freedom to manoeuvre, could
hardly hold the position.

24	♘b5!	♘xb5
25	axb5	a4
26	♗a3	

95
B

It is evident from a glance at
this and the preceding diagram
that the exchanges with the black
pieces defending the e6 square
were in White's favour, and White
has established complete control
here, securing the penetration of
his forces into the enemy position.

| 26 | ... | g6 |
| 27 | ♖e6 | |

Having set up his long-range
artillery in the desired spot, White
has complete control of the open
e-file and threatens 28 ♗xc5.

27	...	♖b8
28	♖ae1	gxf5
29	♖e7	♘xc4+

A gesture of despair, but after
the natural 29 ... ♕d8 30 ♕xf5+
♘d7 Black is helpless.

| 30 | ♕xc4 | ♕xb5 |
| 31 | ♕c2 | |

White prefers to avoid
exchanging his queen as it will be
needed for a direct assault on the
king; now the activity of the black
pieces lasts for two moves only.

| 31 | ... | ♕a5+ |
| 32 | ♔d1 | ♖b3 |

The game continued as follows:
33 ♕xf5+ ♔b8 34 ♖e8+ ♖xe8
35 ♖xe8+ ♔a7 36 ♕d7+ ♖b7
37 ♕xd6 ♖b1+ 38 ♔c2 ♖b2+
39 ♗xb2 **Black resigned.**

Botvinnik–Sorokin
Moscow 1931

96
W

In the preceding example one of
the purposes of the exchanges was
to occupy a file. Where control of
an open file is already secure, the
exchange can be undertaken with
the purpose of realizing this positional advantage. The position
shown in the diagram arose in one
of Botvinnik's early games.

Black, unable to solve the opening problems, is backward in development; the e5 pawn is weak
and, most serious of all, the d-file
is completely in White's hands.

Botvinnik's decision – to exchange queens – seems paradoxical
at first glance.

| 20 | ♕e3 | |

The great importance that the
future World Champion attached
to the question of the exchange

even in those early days is evident
from his expressive comments
regarding the above move: "This
far from obvious move is extremely strong in the given position. With this queen exchange,
which cannot be declined, Black's
positional deficiencies will
become more appreciable.
Because of his backward development, Black has nothing to op-
pose the pressure along the d-file.
The e5 pawn will become very
weak. To defend this pawn, Black
has to exchange his bishop for the
f3 knight, but this will lead to a
weakening not only of his queenside but of the f7 square. So, with
the help of one exchange, it is
possible to force another one with
more serious consequences."

20	**...**	**♛xe3**
21	**fxe3**	**♝g4**
22	**a5**	

Another by-product of the
queen exchange: the black knight
is driven back to an unsatisfactory
position.

22	**...**	**♞c8**
23	**♖c1!**	

This move accomplishes two
objectives: it prepares the invasion of the seventh rank by the
rooks, and it virtually forces a
desired exchange. As pointed out
by Botvinnik, Black would not
succeed in retaining the bishop,
since after 23 ... ♖e8 24 h3 ♝h5
25 ♞h4!, faced with the threat of
26 g4, he would be in an unenvi-
able situation.

23	**...**	**♝xf3**
24	**gxf3**	**♞e7**

97
W

In the transition from the middlegame into a complex ending,
White's advantage has undergone
a transformation. The weakness
of the e5 pawn is no longer appreciable; on the other hand, the
b7 and f7 squares are now vulnerable.

Again, a clear-cut, original decision is required from White in
order to solve the problem of
realizing his advantage. And
Botvinnik chooses a well-tried
weapon – the exchange.

25   ♞d5!

In the case of 25 ... ♞xd5
White is prepared to give up his
bishop in order to acquire a clear
plus in the rook ending: 26 ♝xd5
♞xd5 27 ♖xd5.

25	**...**	**♞c6**
26	**♞xf6+**	**gxf6**
27	**♖d7**	**♖ab8**

After 27 ... ♞xa5 28 ♖cc7 the
weakness at f7 is decisive.

28	**♔f2!**	**♞xa5**
29	**♖cc7**	

The game proceeds in keeping
with White's strategic plan. Black
cannot hold the position even
after simplifications.

29	...	♖bc8
30	♖xf7	♖xc7
31	♖xc7+	♔h8
32	♗d5!	

Botvinnik confidently concluded with a win.

One could have a positional advantage by reason of the opponent's badly-placed piece.

Sometimes this could be the root cause of losing a game. Let us recall Tarrasch's words: "One badly placed piece – the whole game is bad."

We shall consider an expedient which helps to expose the inferior position of the opponent's piece.

Kotov–Taimanov
Zurich 1953

98
W

Throughout the rest of the game Kotov's play is based on the badly-placed knight at a5. Firstly, he exchanges both pairs of rooks along the e-file.

15	♖ae1	♖ae8
16	♗c1	♖xe1
17	♖xe1	♖e8
18	♖xe8	♗xe8

Kotov explains the purpose of these exchanges as follows: "I

could not immediately exploit the unfortunate position of the knight. It was essential to utilize the fact that this knight is cut off from the kingside. In an attack against the king I will have an extra piece." And further, "After the exchange of rooks, as with each subsequent simplification, the *extra piece* will become more and more important."

19	♘h4	a6
20	a4	♕a7
21	♘f5	♗f8
22	♘e4!	

Yet another exchange, again to White's advantage – all strictly to plan.

22	...	♘xe4
23	♗xe4	b6
24	♕d1!	

Having exchanged off active hostile pieces, White goes into attack. Exploiting the unfortunate position of the black knight, he establishes a positive dynamism on the decisive part of the board.

24	...	axb5
25	axb5	♗d7
26	♕h5	♗e6
27	♗f4	♘b3

At last the black knight comes into play, but too late. White has virtually an extra piece on the kingside.

28	♕d1	♕a2
29	h4	♘a1
30	h5	♘c2

The unfortunate knight tries to make up, but now White methodically strengthens his position.

31	♗e5	♕b2
32	♗c7	♘a3

33	♕g4	♕c1+
34	♔g2	♘b1
35	♗f4	

Black is completely lost. A crude mistake accelerates the end: **35 ... ♘d2?? 36 ♕e2 and Black resigned**.

It should be noted that, in practice, the player with a small but lasting positional advantage often strives to strengthen his advantage at first, and only then goes for a beneficial exchange.

Ljubojevic–Karpov
Linares 1981

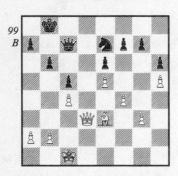

99
B

Black has a microscopic positional advantage. The knight has better prospects than the bishop in such positions, whilst White's control of the d-file has no particular significance since his queen is unable to exploit it with an intrusion. Black intends to exchange queens, but at the present moment such a plan would be premature. Firstly, it is necessary to increase his positional advantage by creating a weakness in White's kingside pawn structure.

| 28 | ... | g6! |

| 29 | hxg6 | fxg6 |
| 30 | a3 | a5! |

Depriving his opponent of counterplay on the queenside.

31	b3	h5
32	♕e4	♘f5
33	♗f2	♕d7

Having activated his forces to the maximum, Karpov seizes control of the open file.

| 34 | a4 | ♔c7! |

Black brings his king into the battle, without fear of any ghosts. On the apparently dangerous intrusion of the white queen 35 ♕a8, there follows: 35 ... ♕d3! 36 ♕a7+ ♔c8 37 ♕a8+ ♔d7 38 ♕b7+ ♔e8 38 ♕b8+ ♔f7 40 ♕b7+ ♘e7 and the black king is safely on the kingside, with profit.

| 35 | ♔c2 | ♕d8! |

Preparing the important breakthrough g6–g5 with subsequent activation of the queen.

36	♔c1	g5
37	fxg5	♕xg5+
38	♔c2	♘e7!

38 ... ♘xg3 would only result in a draw: 39 ♗xg3 ♕xg3 40 ♕h7+ and 41 ♕xh5.

| 39 | ♕h7 | ♔d7! |

A queen exchange would have been feasible now, but Black prefers to go for it under more favourable circumstances.

| 40 | ♕e4 (100) | |

Compare this position with that shown in the previous diagram: the broken-up white pawns are excellent targets for the black knight. It is time to exchange queens.

| 40 | ... | ♕f5 |

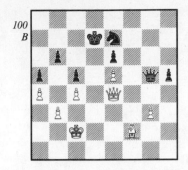

100
B

41	♕d3+	♔c6
42	♕xf5	exf5
43	♗e3	♘g6
44	e6	♔d6
45	♗g5	

The e-pawn is doomed. An attempt by the bishop to attack the black pawns on the queenside is too slow.

45	...	♔xe6
46	♔d3	f4!
47	gxf4	h4
48	♔e3	h3
49	♔f3	♔f5
50	♔g3	

The passed pawn is detained, but Black produces a decisive blow.

| 50 | ... | ♘xf4! |

Offering to exchange the remaining pieces: 51 ♗xf4 h2 52 ♔xh2 ♔xf4 and White is in a hopeless situation in the pawn endgame.

51	♗d8	♘e2+
52	♔xh3	♘d4
53	♗xb6	♘xb3

Although the number of pawns on the board has diminished, White's position has not become any easier. The active black king quickly resolved the outcome: **54**

♗d8 ♔e4 55 ♔g4 ♔d4 56 ♔f4 ♔xc4 57 ♔e4 ♔c3! 58 ♗f6+ ♔c2 59 ♗e5 c4 60 ♔e3 c3 61 ♗f6 ♘c5 62 ♔e2 ♔b3 White resigned.

Unequal or Non-Identical Exchanges

In most fields of professional activity the accumulation of theoretical knowledge and practical experience gives rise to stock phrases, and although this jargon remains in general use it does not always correspond to varying shades of the phenomenon it purports to describe.

Such clichés exist in chess too. Many times the reader has probably read of events in the course of a game described rather emotively, such as "And here I sacrificed my queen for two rooks" or "It was necessary to sacrifice a rook for a bishop and two pawns." Is it correct to use the term *sacrifice* in these situations? Obviously, if it is a question of parting with the queen without material compensation, then indeed this is a sacrifice, but when an exchange of material of similar value takes place, one cannot specify whether or not there was a definite material loss. In chess literature the word *exchange* is generally used in a more specific sense than the usual meaning of the word. Here it is regarded as the consecutive elimination of equal pieces from each side. For example, a bishop and a knight differ sharply from each other in their characteristics, but their absolute value is about the same.

In mathematics there are two closely related concepts: equality and identity. Using this terminology it is possible to distinguish between two types of exchange: identical, involving the exchange of equal pieces, and non-identical, the exchange of material of approximately equal *abstract* value but differing in *concrete* value in a given situation.

The question of identical exchanges has been mentioned in some form or other in many works dealing with middlegame and endgame theory.

However, the non-identical exchange, which occurs quite frequently in practice, has clearly evaded the notice of theoreticians. The rôle of the non-identical exchange is significant not just from the practical, sporting point of view, but also for an aesthetic perception of chess.

Not surprisingly the question is sometimes asked: "What do you regard as the beauty of chess?" The following answer is given by Botvinnik, an outstanding authority on creative chess: "Beautiful games can only take place between masters, since they exchange not only the average, invariable value of the piece, but also its real value, corresponding to the real strength of the piece at a given moment in the game. The average value is obvious, the real value is hidden. Only a deep analysis can reveal the real value of a piece. This depth of analysis gives an aesthetically satisfying sensation to the chessplaying public."

Non-identical exchanges are heterogeneous – in the material exchanged, in their mode of formation and in their strategic aims. But they all lead to an atypical or heterogeneous dynamism on the chessboard.

The course of action to be followed in a position with dynamic imbalance arises in the chessplayer's imagination associated with his ability to operate in positions without clear-cut guidelines.

There is a school of thought that creative chessplayers are not fond of dry, technical positions. Alas, nothing is further from the truth. Perhaps it is inappropriate here to enlarge on the importance of understanding technical positions. This is axiomatic. In an endgame struggle with a dynamic imbalance it may seem that concrete technical knowledge is relatively unimportant, yet it is precisely here that its rôle is elevated. Successfully conducting a complex endgame with a dynamic imbalance can only be carried out by a fusion of imagination and workaday play. It is precisely an accurate technical insight into the ensuing – albeit hypothetical – position that serves as a guiding light to the player, showing the correct path to follow. In such a situation the rôle of the exchange is the vital link connecting two positions of entirely different character.

I believe the time has come for an investigation into positions with a dynamic imbalance. Until quite recently the problems associated with such positions were of relatively little importance, whereas in contemporary chess, with the constant growth of dynamic play and the tireless search for new lines in apparently well-investigated systems, their rôle is becoming crucial.

One should consider that in the endgame a whole series of such positions, with their unequal alignment of forces, has been studied. Quite a number of these so-called technical endgame positions are simply essential for a chessplayer to know. They are distinct objectives, helping the player to plan his game, as mentioned by Krogius in his book *Principles of the Endgame*.

In contrast to technical endgames, there has been considerably less study of middlegame problems under conditions of dynamic imbalance, and *their* systematization is practically non-existent.

There is also a series of modern opening systems involving non-identical exchanges, in which play proceeds with a dynamic imbalance.

We recall Spielmann's words from his book *Theory of the Sacrifice*—"... All chess pieces have two

values: an absolute and a relative value. The simpler the position, the greater the significance of the absolute value, whereas the more intricate the position, the greater is the significance of the relative value. The absolute value of a piece is a guide – it is of constant magnitude, in contrast to the relative value, which is variable and transient." The relative value of a piece is an important criterion in non-identical exchanges.

Owing to the rapid growth of opening theory in recent years, chessplayers are required to adopt a creative approach to opening problems. One way of searching for new forms of opening play is to create in the early stages of the game a position with dynamic imbalance, accomplished with the aid of non-identical exchanges.

The opportunities for disrupting material identity between the two sides in well-known opening variations, casting off from established lines of play and giving a romantic quality to the game, evinces prospects of such an approach to the opening.

In his book *The Opening and the Middlegame* Grandmaster Suetin writes: "... In our times there has been a significant growth in the number of opening variations with a heterogeneous material relationship. They are not of minor importance; they originate during play in the most highly principled aspirations of the players, in a series of opening systems." The results of the struggle in such opening variations is problematic.

There is a whole series of opening systems in which play proceeds with an unequal alignment of forces.

If we consider that, in planning the initial stages of the game, and experienced player will try and anticipate the character of the ensuing struggle, then the problems encountered here will be particularly interesting.

In practically all, even the most orthodox openings, it is possible to discover a series of systems or variations with dynamic imbalance.

Pereira–Nesis
11th World Correspondence
Championship 1983/7

1	d4	♘f6
2	♘f3	g6
3	♗f4	♗g7
4	♘c3	d6
5	e4	♘c6
6	♕d2	0-0
7	0-0-0	♗g4

With a transposition of moves the game has reached a rare variation of the Pirc–Ufimsev defence, in which castling on opposite sides of the board promises sharp play.

8	♕e3	♘d7
9	e5	dxe5
10	♗xe5	♘dxe5
11	dxe5	♕c8

| 12 | ♘d5 | ♕e6! |

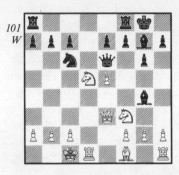

101 W

Black offers the sacrifice of the exchange: 13 ♘xc7 ♕xa2, after which the white king is in a predicament. However, it appears that White has another possibility of refuting his adversary's plans. He can win the black queen.

13	♗c4	♗xf3!
14	♘f6+	

White could not back down, otherwise he would lose the e5 pawn.

14	...	exf6
15	♗xe6	♗xd1
16	♗h3	

Black has a rook and two minor pieces for the queen. But his light-squared bishop could fall into an ambush, as on 16 ... ♗h5 there follows 17 g4. However, the doomed bishop gives up its life dearly.

16	...	♗xc2!
17	♔xc2	

The intermediate move 17 exf6 ♗xf6 18 ♔xc2 is followed by 18 ... ♖fe8!

17	...	fxe5
18	♔b1	♘d4

19	♖c1	c6
20	g3	a5
21	a4	♖a6!

As a result of the tactical operation carried out in the opening, Black acquired more than sufficient material and positional compensation for his queen. Since there is a possibility of organizing an attack against the white king, his chances are distinctly the better.

22	♖c5	♖b6
23	♕e1	♘b3
24	♖c4	

The best defence. 24 ♖xa5 e4 25 ♖g5 ♖d8! with a decisive initiative. On 24 ♖c2, ... ♖b4 is strong.

| 24 | ... | ♖d8 |
| 25 | ♔a2 | |

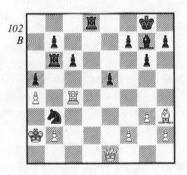

102
B

| 25 | ... | e4! |

An unexpected move. Black sacrifices his central pawn to bring about a rook exchange, intensifying the opponent's problem of defending his queen's wing.

26	♖xe4	♘c5
27	♖e8+	♖xe8
28	♕xe8+	♗f8

Despite approximate material equality, it is difficult for the white queen to resist against the harmoniously placed black pieces.

| 29 | ♗f5!? | |

An interesting tactical stroke, the purpose of which is the transfer of the bishop to defend the king. If 29 ... gxf5, then 30 ♕d8! and the queen would demonstrate superiority, aiming both for the rook on the queenside as well as the g5 square, so that Black could not avoid perpetual check.

| 29 | ... | ♘xa4 |
| 30 | b3 | ♘c3+ |

30 ... ♘c5 is weaker – 31 ♗c2 and White's defence would have firmed up.

| 31 | ♔b2 | ♘d5 |
| 32 | ♗d3 | |

The bishop is heading for the c4 square in order to, together with the queen, take aim at f7, pinning the dangerous knight.

32	...	a4
33	♗c4	♖b4
34	♔a1	b5!
35	♗xd5	cxd5

The formidable knight has been exchanged, but there is no question regarding Black's superiority.

36	bxa4	bxa4
37	f4	a3
38	f5	♖b2
39	h4	gxf5

and Black's advantage was decisive.

Of the modern opening variations in which a position arises with pawn compensation for a minor piece, or even for a rook, one immediately thinks of the Yugoslav Attack in the Dragon Variation of the Sicilian Defence.

Lekrok–Nesis
11th Correspondence World Cup

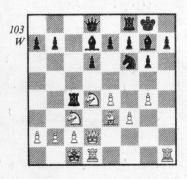

In this position White has a choice of several continuations. For a long time 16 ♘de2 was considered to be a most menacing move. The knight retreats from a square where it might have come under attack, and protects the other knight on c3. White now threatens the typical manoeuvre 17 e5 dxe5 18 g5.

16 ♘de2   ♖e8!

In this way Black saves his king's bishop from the exchange, but at the same time commits himself to giving up his knight for three pawns.

16 ... ♕a5 is weaker – 17 ♗h6 ♗xh6 18 ♕xh6 ♖fc8 19 ♖d3! with definite pressure.

17 ♗h6

The immediate 17 e5 is premature, in view of 17 ... ♘xg4! 18 fxg4 ♗xg4 and Black has three pawns for the knight, with active opportunities. For example, 19

exd6 ♕xd6 20 ♕e1?! ♗xc3! or 20 ♕xd6 exd6 and the white bishop on e3 is under attack. Evidently, White's best chance is 19 e6!? ♗xe6 20 ♗d4 (Strand–Nikhitel, Correspondence 1984).

17 ...   ♗h8
18 e5

White accepts the challenge. Passive play would give him very little. For instance, 18 ♕e1 b5! 19 b3 ♖c8 20 ♔b1 ♕a5 21 ♗c1 b4 22 ♘d5 ♖xc2! 23 ♘xb4 ♖xe2 24 ♕xe2 ♕xb4 with a clear advantage for Black (Hartston–Sosonko, Hastings 1975/6).

18 ...   ♘xg4
19 fxg4   ♗xe5

It is important to eliminate the e5 pawn.

In the case of 19 ... ♗xg4 20 exd6! ♕xd6 21 ♕xd6 exd6 22 ♖xd6, White has the advantage. For instance: 22 ... ♗g7 23 ♗xg7 ♔xg7 24 ♘d4 h5 25 ♔d2 ♖cc8 26 ♔d3 ♖cd8 27 ♖xd8 ♖xd8 28 ♘e4 ♗f5 29 c3 ♔h6 30 ♖f1 h4 31 ♔e3 (Beliavsky–Filguth, Caracas 1977), and in view of the great activity of the white king, the extra piece is stronger in the endgame than the three pawns.

20 ♗f4

A well-known attempt to maintain the tension in such a dynamically unbalanced situation would lie in the following continuation: 20 ♘d5 ♗xg4 21 ♘e3 ♖a4 22 ♘xg4 ♖xg4 and Black now has four pawns for the minor piece; however, White can exchange Black's important light-squared bishop and, in the ensuing struggle, Black has to play sensitively: 23 ♖df1 ♕b6 24 c3 ♕c6 25 ♗e3 h5 26 ♖hg1! ♖xg1 27 ♖xg1 a6 28 ♕d3 ♗g7 29 ♘f4 ♕b5 (Kutianin–Nesis, Soviet Correspondence Championship 1977/8).

20	...	♕a5
21	♗xe5	♕xe5
22	♘d5	

Until the present game this had been regarded as the strongest move. White gives up a fourth pawn for the minor piece to acquire strong pressure in the centre. Other attempts have been made with the purpose of retaining the g-pawn: 22 g5 b5! 23 ♘d4 b4 24 ♘ce2 ♖ec8 25 ♖h4 ♗a4! 26 b3 ♖xc2+! 27 ♕xc2 ♕xg5+ 28 ♖f4 ♖xc2+ 29 ♔xc2 e5 (Eizen–Nesis, Correspondence Match, USSR versus USA 1980/2). Although White has many pieces for his queen, the black pawn army sweeps all obstacles from its path. For instance, 30 ♖g1 ♕h5! 31 ♖f2 exd4 32 bxa4 ♕c5+ with 9 subsequent d4–d3. The game with Eizen continued: 30 ♖ff1 ♗d7 31 ♘f3 ♗f5+ 32 ♔b2 ♕g2 and the white pieces are completely helpless. After 34 ♔h4 ♕e4 White resigned. White could have played more precisely – 22 ♕h6 ♕g7 23 g5 ♗c6 24 ♖h3 ♕xh6 25 ♖xh6 ♖g4 26 ♘d4 ♔g7 (Zborovsky–Nesis, 13th Soviet Correspondence Championship 1977/8), although here also Black has better prospects in the endgame.

| 22 | ... | ♖xg4 |

| 23 | ♘ec3 | ♕g5 |

A queen exchange is more profitable to the side with the pawn majority.

| 24 | ♖de1 | |

This move is more subtle than 24 ♖he1 ♔f8! 25 ♘e3 ♖h4 26 ♘cd5 ♗c6 27 ♕c3 ♕e5 (Klovans–Beliavsky, Leningrad 1977).

| 24 | ... | h5! |

In the absence of queens this meek little pawn becomes a monster. 24 ... ♗c6 would have been somewhat weaker – 25 ♕xg5 ♖xg5 26 ♖xe7 ♖xe7 27 ♘xe7+ ♔g7 28 ♖d1 h5 29 ♘xc6! (Georgiev–Sekveira, Innsbruck 1977).

| 25 | ♕xg5 | ♖xg5 |
| 26 | ♘xe7+ | ♔g7! |

Black must be on the alert now that the queens have been exchanged. 26 ... ♔f8 would have been a mistake: 27 ♘ed5 ♖xe1+ 28 ♖xe1 and 28 ... h4? is bad because of 29 ♘f6

| 27 | ♘ed5 | ♖xe1+ |
| 28 | ♖xe1 | h4! |

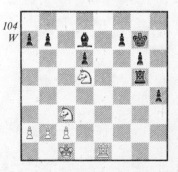

104
W

So a popular opening variation has been forcefully led into an ending with an unusual advantage relationship. Black has given up a minor piece for three pawns, and despite approximate material equality, White's position is hopeless. He has nothing to counter the rapidly advancing pawn trio supported by the long-range bishop.

29	♘e3	♗c6

Black takes aim at the h1 square.

30	♖e2	d5
31	♖d2	h3
32	♘cd1	d4!

And the formerly weak d-pawn has a sting. On 33 ♖xd4, 33 ... h2 is decisive.

33	♘f1	♖g1
34	♘h2	f5
35	♖f2	

In the case of 35 ♖d3, 35 ... ♗e4! 36 ♖xh3 ♖g2 wins.

35	...	♚f6

Finally, the king enters the battle.

36	c3	dxc3
37	bxc3	♗a4
38	♖f1	♖xf1
39	♘xf1	♗xd1

In such positions, exchanges are the quickest way to victory.

40	♚xd1	g5
41	♚e2	g4
42	♚f2	f4

A complete triumph for the pawns in their battle against the knight.

43	♘d2	g3+

White resigned.

The emergence of positions with a dynamic imbalance is characteristic of sharp opening systems, such as the Dutch Defence.

Ribli–Barber
Lugano 1985
Dutch Defence

1	♘f3	f5
2	g3	♘f6
3	♗g2	g6
4	0-0	♗g7
5	c4	0-0
6	d4	d6
7	♘c3	♘c6
8	d5	♘e5
9	♘xe5	dxe5
10	♕b3	

Also possible is 10 e4 f4. For instance, 11 gxf4 exf4 12 e5 ♘g4 13 e6 ♘e5 14 ♕b3 f3 15 ♗h3 g5 16 ♖e1 g4 17 ♗f1 ♕e8 18 ♘e4 ♕h5 19 ♕e3 h6 20 ♗d2 ♘g6 21 ♗c3 and White stands better (Ivanka–Lazarevic, Medellin 1974).

Or 11 b4 g5 12 ♖e1 a6 13 ♗b2 ♕e8 14 c5! ♗d7 and now 15 c6! bxc6 16 dxc6 ♗xc6 17 ♘d5! and White has a definite advantage (Hansen–Christiansen, Ejsberg 1984).

10	...	e6
11	♖d1	exd5
12	♘xd5	c6
13	♗g5!?	

An interesting innovation. The exchange 13 ♘xf6+ ♕xf6 leads only to equality.

13	...	cxd5

After 13 ... ♕a5 14 ♘e7+ ♚h8 15 ♘xc8 ♖axc8 16 ♕xb7 wins a pawn.

| 14 | ♗xd5+ | ♔h8 |
| 15 | ♗xb7 | ♕xd1+ |

A dubious decision. 15 ... ♗d7 is also bad – 16 ♗xa8 ♕xa8 17 ♗xf6 ♗xf6 18 ♖xd7, but after 15 ... ♖b8! 16 ♗xd8 ♖xd8 17 ♖d1 ♖g8! (*as 17 ... ♖xd1? 18 ♕xd1 ♗xb7 19 ♗xf6 ♗xf6 20 ♕d6 wins. 17 ... ♖e8 is also bad, because of 18 ♕a4!*) 18 ♕a3 ♖xb7 and the outcome of the game is unclear.

| 16 | ♖xd1 | ♖b8 |
| 17 | ♕a3 | ♗xb7 |

Naturally not 17 ... ♖xb7?, because of 18 ♗xf6.

18	♗xf6	♗xf6
19	♕xa7	♗a8
20	b3	

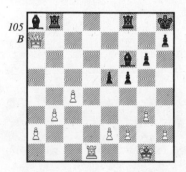

105
B

We now have an unusual alignment of forces: queen and three pawns against a rook and two bishops. In spite of approximate material equality, White's advantage is obvious. As we have said, as a result of the recent extraordinary growth of opening theory, chessplayers are required to adopt a creative, original approach to opening problems. One such approach is to create a dynamic imbalance in the early stages of the game. Recall what Suetin said: "In our times there has been a significant growth in the number of opening variations with a heterogeneous material relationship. They are not of minor importance; they originate during play in the most highly principled aspirations of the players, in a series of opening systems."

Such systems abound in the Dutch Defence.

20	...	♖bd8
21	♖xd8	♖xd8
22	f3	e4

More stubborn would have been 22 ... ♔g8.

23	♕f7	♗d4+
24	♔g2	exf3+
25	exf3	♗g7
26	♕e7	♖f8
27	b4	h5

Black has difficulty in improving the coordination of his pieces, and the passed pawns on the queenside are unstoppable.

28	b5	♔g8
29	b6	♗f6
30	♕e6+	♔g7
31	c5	♖d8
32	c6	♖d2+
33	♔f1	f4
34	b7	

Black resigned.

The problems arising in situations with atypical imbalances must be the subject of a separate study.

We show just a few examples involving the exchange of the most powerful piece – the queen –

for various pieces, maintaining rough material equality.

Naturally, we have in mind the generally accepted arithmetical scale used for calculating the comparative values of the chess pieces: Queen–9 points; rook–5 points; minor piece–3 points; pawn–1 point.

Although this scale is a determining criterion in appraising the position, it is not always applicable to a conclusive evaluation of a game in progress.

Geller–Ivkov
Beverley 1965

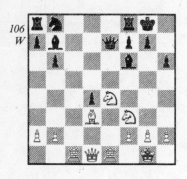

106
W

15   ♘c5   ♛xc5

Efim Geller comments on this game: "Finding himself in a difficult position, Black parts with his queen, exchanging it for equivalent material. The heterogeneity of pieces remaining on the board demands energetic play from White, possibly the only way left for him to proceed. This is usually the case in a struggle of the queen against several other pieces. In such cases the reliability of the

king's cover, the presence and extent of advance of passed pawns is of particular importance." These observations of the experienced Grandmaster are most important for understanding the problems encountered in the battle of the queen against pieces.

16   ♖xc5   bxc5

So Black has equivalent material for his queen – a rook, a bishop and a passed pawn. White is required to take the initiative.

17   ♘e5!

With this move, White hinders his opponent's development on the queenside and forces the exchange of his strong bishop.

17   ...   ♗xe5

As pointed out by Geller, after 17 ... ♖e8, strong is 18 ♘g4 ♘d7 19 ♖xe8+ ♖xe8 20 ♗b5 ♗c8 (*20 ... ♖d8 is bad, in view of 21 ♗xd7 ♖xd7 22 ♘xf6+ and 23 ♛g4+*) 21 ♘xf6+ gxf6 22 h3 with a clear advantage for White.

18	**♖xe5**	**♘d7**
19	**♖e7**	**♗c6**
20	**h3**	**♖ae8**

Black has defended himself from any immediate threats. If he now succeeds in exchanging the white bishop, the d4 pawn will become dangerous.

White's task is to organize an attack against the black king.

21	**♛e1**	**♘b6**
22	**b3**	

Firstly, White blocks the advance of the c5 pawn.

22	**...**	**♘d5**
23	**♖xe8+**	**♖xe8**

24 ♕c1

The apparently active 24 ♕a5 is answered by 24 ... ♘f4!

24 ... ♘c3

25 ♔h2

A subtle move. White leaves the first rank with his king to free his queen and deprive Black of active opportunities.

25 ... ♖d8

Black decides to play for the d4 pawn.

26 ♕f4 ♘d5

27 ♕f5

White has succeeded in setting up a strong battery on the diagonal. However, in Geller's opinion, 27 ♕e5 ♘b4 28 ♕c7 would have been more accurate.

27 ... ♘b4

If 27 ... g6 28 ♕e5 ♘b4 29 ♗c4 d3 30 ♕f6 with a strong initiative.

Black offers a pawn sacrifice in order to exchange White's blockading bishop: 28 ♕xc5 ♘xd3 29 ♕xc6 ♘f4 and the d-pawn would give Black excellent chances of success.

28 ♕h7+ ♔f8

29 ♗c4

Threatening ♕h8+

29 ... ♗d5

Black tries to exchange the white bishop at any price.

30 ♗f1 f6

This is the only way Black can save his g7 pawn.

Now 31 ♕h8+ is bad – 31 ... ♗g8 32 ♗c4 ♘d5! and the queen has unexpectedly fallen into a trap.

31 a3!

White drives away Black's knight, depriving him of the above tactical opportunity.

31 ... ♘a2

32 ♕h8+ ♔e7

33 ♕xg7+ ♗f7

34 ♗c4 ♖f8

35 ♕h7!

The queen, simultaneously keeping the pin on the bishop and Black's passed pawn under control, demonstrates her dexterity.

35 ... ♘c3

36 ♕f5 ♗xc4

The white queen has succeeded in breaking the coordination of the black pieces.

37 ♕xc5+ ♔e6

38 ♕xc4+ ♔e5

In a hopeless position and in time trouble, Black loses his rook.

39 ♕c5+

and after two moves **Black resigned**.

Oll–Ubilava
Moscow 1983

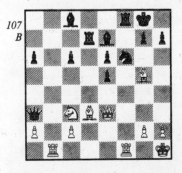

It is not difficult to work out that this sharp position came about after a ramification of the Najdorf Variation of the Sicilian

Defence. Black has two extra pawns but White has a fairly strong threat on the kingside: on 18 ... ♜d4, 19 ♗xf6, followed by 20 ♘e2 is strong.

To minimize his young opponent's attacking potential, the experienced Grandmaster decides to exchange his queen for three minor pieces.

18 ...   ♛xc3!?

19 ♗xh7 +

The preliminary 19 ♗xf6 would be bad, because of 19 ... ♜xd3 20 ♗xe7 ♜xf1+ 21 ♜xf1 ♜d1!

19 ...   ♘xh7

20 ♛xc3   ♗xg5

Capturing the bishop with the knight would have been weaker: 20 ... ♘xg5 21 ♜xf8+ ♗xf8 22 ♛xc6 ♜d8 23 ♛c7 ♜e8 24 ♜b8 ♗d7 25 ♜xe8 ♗xe8 26 ♛d8.

A preliminary rook exchange would not be any better: 20 ... ♜xf1+ 21 ♜xf1 ♘xg5 22 ♛xc6 ♜d8 23 ♛c7 ♜e8 24 ♛xe5.

White would have the advantage in both cases.

21 ♛xe5

108
B

In a struggle between non-identical material, the effect of any exchange is extremely significant. The point is that in a situation of dynamic imbalance the relative value of the pieces carries greater weight than their absolute value. So the geometrical nature of the pieces remaining after the exchange must be looked at. For instance, when the kings are well-protected, the queen and knight combination is usually stronger than two rooks and a bishop. After the exchange of the knight for the bishop, however, a pair of rooks is a formidable force in a battle against the queen.

21 ...   ♜xf1 +

The Estonian masters Oll and Veingold made the following comments regarding this mistaken exchange: "A positional blunder. After the exchange of one pair of rooks, it is difficult for Black to actively coordinate his pieces in the absence of such reliable buttresses as the two rooks. On the other hand, 21 ... ♜fe8! with subsequent ♗f6 and e6–e5 would have given Black the opportunity of setting up a reliable configuration, enabling him to liquidate his opponent's aggression. In this case the possibility of Black advancing the passed e-pawn would have given White some difficult problems." Here we see the significance of just one exchange in a struggle between non-identical material.

22 ♜xf1   ♜d8

22 ... ♜e7 is too passive – 23 ♛d6 ♗d7 24 g3 and with the

subsequent idea of 25 h4, the black pieces would be suffocated within their own camp.

23 ♕c7

The white queen bursts into the heart of the enemy camp, not allowing any breathing space.

23 ... ♗d7
24 ♖d1 ♘f8
25 ♕a5

Exploiting the disharmonious arrangement of his opponent's forces, White captures a pawn and, more importantly, creates his own distant passed pawn.

25 ... ♗f6
26 ♕xa6 e5
27 ♕a7

It was worth considering the more decisive 27 a4.

27 ... e4
28 ♔g1 ♗g5
29 ♕c5 ♗h6

In the case of 29 ... ♘e6, 30 ♕c4 is strong, with 31 ♖xd7 threatening to capture Black's only remaining hope – the e-pawn.

30 g4

A rash decision. An unusual balance of forces requires unusual decisions. Just one move with the queen would have left White with a clear advantage – 30 ♕e7! After the obvious 30 ... ♖e8, White would have unexpectedly given up his queen for a rook and a bishop, but in the ending his rook and the passed a-pawn would have been stronger than Black's two minor pieces: 31 ♖xd7! ♖xe7 32 ♖xe7. An interesting case of transform-

ing a heterogeneous situation!

30 ... ♗f4

Black's play is also ill-judged. 30 ... e3!? should have been considered – 31 g5 e2 32 ♖e1 ♘e6 33 ♕c4 ♗xg5 34 ♖xe2 ♔f7, or 32 ♕c4+ ♔h8 33 ♖xe2 ♗xg5.

31 ♖f1 g5

More stubborn would have been 31 ... ♘e6.

32 ♖xf4!

A beautiful example of a positional sacrifice of the exchange. Now the queen will be left to fight alone against a rook and two minor pieces. But the black king will soon be in difficulties.

32 ... ♘e6

Naturally not 32 ... gxf4 33 ♕g5+

33 ♕e7! gxf4
34 g5 ♗c8
35 g6 ♖d1+
36 ♔f2

36 ♔g2 would be a mistake in view of 36 ... f3+ 37 ♔f2 ♖d2+ 38 ♔e1 f2+! and the black pawn would not only be promoted to queen but would then defend f7, which is White's intended mating square.

36 ... e3+
37 ♔f3?

Play can be incredibly complex in a heterogeneous game especially in a hazardous position.

In such situations, general principles do not apply; every move is crucial. Inevitably, this takes up a lot of the players' time. So the final stages of this unusual type of game are often played with both sides under time pressure; consequently a great number of mistakes are committed. This game is no exception.

After the text move there was a problem-like opportunity for Black to save the game: 37 ... ♖f1+! 38 ♔e4 (*a draw is also reached by 38 ♔g2 ♖f2+ 39 ♔g1 ♘g5! 40 ♕xg5 ♗h3!*) 38 ... ♘g5+! 39 ♔e5 e2 40 ♔f6 ♘e4+! and White must accept a draw by repetition: 41 ♔e5 ♘g5, since on 41 ♕xe4 there follows 41 ... e1(♕).

Because this drawing opportunity was available to Black, White should have lured the rook on to the second rank: 37 ♔e2! ♖d2+ 38 ♔f3 ♖f2+ 39 ♔e4 ♘g5+ 40 ♔e5 e2 41 ♔f6 and now the above variation is no longer appropriate, as the e-pawn's promotion square is undefended by the rook.

However, it is gruelling to evaluate all these variations under time pressure, and Black missed his opportunity.

37	...	♘d4+
38	♔xf4	♖f1+
39	♔e4	♘e6

Black has stopped the mate, but in losing his only trump cards in the battle against the queen – his passed pawns – his position becomes hopeless.

| 40 | ♔xe3 | c5 |
| 41 | ♕h7+ | ♔f8 |

| 42 | ♕h8+ |

Black resigned.

Velimirovic–Popovic

Yugoslavian Championship 1986

The f7 square is so hopelessly weak that White could simply play 15 ♗xf7+ ♔h8 16 ♕c3 ♕xc3 17 ♗xc3 ♗d7, but in this event Black could hold on in the endgame. The Yugoslavian Grandmaster is known as a great chess romantic and prefers a combinative course of action: he sacrifices his queen, anticipating compensation for it in subsequent play.

| 15 | ♕xf7+! | ♖xf7 |
| 16 | ♖xf7 | ♘e5 |

16 ... d5 is bad, on account of 17 ♖xe7 ♔f8 18 ♗c5 ♕xc5 19 ♘xc5 ♔xe7 20 ♗xd5 and White has an extra pawn for which Black has no compensation.

| 17 | ♗xe5! |

In the case of the immediate 17 ♖xe7+ ♔f8 the white rook is in a trap.

17	...	dxe5
18	♖xe7+	♔f8
19	♖f7+	♔g8

An original mill has emerged; after 19 ... ♔e8 20 ♘d6+ ♔d8 21 ♖d1 with decisive threats.

| 20 | ♖f6+ | ♗e6 |

On 20 ... ♔h8 21 ♖f8 mate.

| 21 | ♖xe6 | ♔h8 |
| 22 | ♖f1 | h6 |

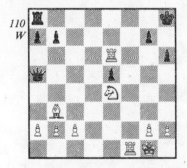

As a result of the combinative attack, White has acquired a large material advantage: rook, knight, bishop and pawn for a queen. But one should not forget that the queen remains a queen, particularly in positions where many of the opponent's pieces do not coordinate harmoniously.

| 23 | c3 | |

23 ♘d6 should have been considered.

23	...	♖d8
24	♖f7	♕b5
25	h3	a5

After the aggressive 25 ... ♕e2 26 ♘d6 with a winning attack.

| 26 | ♖xh6+? | |

But this combination is a mistake. White could have realized his advantage by positional means. For instance: 26 ♖ee7 a4 27 ♗e6 (27 ♖xg7! ♕b6+) 27 ... ♕xb2 28 ♔h2 or 26 ♖f5 a4 27 ♖fxe5 ♕d3 28 ♖e8+

26	...	gxh6
27	♘f6	♕d3
28	♘g4	e4
29	♖e7	♖f8
30	♘e5	♕f1+

The queen, which not long ago was passive, shows her superiority.

| 31 | ♔h2 | ♕f4+ |
| 32 | ♔g1 | ♕e3+ |

An interesting case of a positional draw. Black already has a material advantage of the queen for two minor pieces and a pawn, but the teetering position of his king forces him to accept.

| 33 | ♔h2 | ♕f4+ |
| 34 | ♔g1 | ♕e3+ |

Drawn.

The following is an example of two rooks operating together successfully.

Letich–Dunhaupt
Correspondence 1980/2

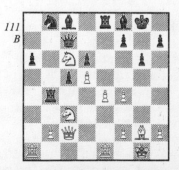

We have here a tense, double-edged situation, characteristic of the Benoni. White is poised to advance in the centre, while Black exerts pressure on the e- and b- pawns. And yet White seems to be ahead in development: he is attacking Black's pride and joy – the rook at b4 – and threatens the thematic thrust e4–e5.

26 ...   ♗d7!

27 ♗f1!?

An unusual decision! Naturally, 27 ♘xb4 cxb4 is bad because White loses two knights for a rook. If 27 ♘xb8 ♖xb8, then Black's pressure would become unbearable. In Dunhaupt's estimation, the consequences of this bishop finesse will come to light only after the non-identical exchange of two rooks for a queen.

27 ...   ♘xc6

28 dxc6   ♗xc6

29 ♖xa6   ♕b7!

30 ♖xc6

This tactical thrust is part of White's plan. However, Black willingly takes up the challenge.

30 ...   ♕xc6

31 ♘d5

An original attack on both black rooks: the threats are 32 ♘xb4 or 32 ♘f6+. But ...

31 ...   ♕xd5!

32 exd5   ♖xe1

The rook penetrates to the first rank, but without a check in consequence of White's strange move 27 ♗f1!? Nevertheless, the two black rooks are clearly stronger than the white queen.

The presence of opposite-coloured bishops is also in Black's favour; but it is important that the black pieces work in concert.

33 f3

The purpose of this move is temporarily to defend the f4 pawn. 33 f5? is impossible because of 33 ... ♖g4+. Also 33 ♕d2 is not helpful on account of 33 ... ♖b1.

33 ...   ♗g7

The immediate 33 ... ♖xf4? would be answered by 34 ♕d2.

34 b3   ♖xf4!

But now if 35 ♕d2 ♖e3!; or Black may embark on yet another non-identical exchange: 35 ... ♖xf1+ 36 ♔xf1 ♖xf3+ 37 ♔g2 ♖xb3 with decisive threats.

35 ♔f2   ♖a1!

A subtle move, forcing the white bishop to remain on the first rank. For instance, 36 ♗e2 ♗d4+ 37 ♔g2 ♖g1+, or 36 ♗h3 ♗d4! with subsequent ... ♖ad1 or 36 ♗c4 ♗d4+ 37 ♔e2 ♖h1.

36 ♕e2   ♗d4+

37 ♔g2   ♖b1

The queen is powerless against the fury of the rooks. For instance, 38 ♕d3 ♖b2+ 39 ♗e2 ♖f5! threatening 40 ... ♖g5+ or 40 ... ♖e5, and if the king moves to the h-file – 39 ♔h1 or ♔h3 – then the ambush 39 ... ♗e5 is decisive. The futile check 38 ♕e8+ ♔g7 would leave the white king defenceless.

White resigned.

The author has persevered with the thesis that in modern,

dynamic chess, positions with a heterogeneous alignment of forces are a frequent occurrence, sometimes with the disruption of material equality – or, more precisely, of material identity – taking place in the early stages.

To confirm this we show every game of the 13th round in the top league of the 1987 Soviet Championships, the main forum of Russian chess, for which competition I had the occasion to write the commentary.

Lputian–Beliavsky
Minsk 1987

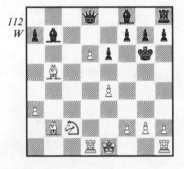

112
W

This highly unusual position – note the placing of the black king! – arose after only 17 moves. How did such an irrational situation come about? After the book moves of the Petrosian Variation of the Queen's Indian Defence: **1 d4 ♘f6 2 c4 e6 3 ♘f3 b6 4 ♘c3 ♗b7 5 a3 d5 6 cxd5 ♘xd5 7 ♕c2 c5 8 e4 ♘xc3 9 bxc3 ♘c6 10 ♗b2 cxd4 11 cxd4 ♖c8 12 ♖d1**, Beliavsky embarked on a new line – **12 ... b5!?**, the usual continuation 12 ... a6 having been refuted

by 13 ♕d2 ♘a5 14 d5! with a strong attack (Kasparov–Murey, Moscow 1982).

In reply, Lputian went for an interesting though somewhat questionable queen sacrifice: **13 d5 ♘d4 14 ♘xd4 ♖xc2 15 ♗xb5+ ♔e7 16 d6+ ♔f6 17 ♘xc2 ♔g6**, and we have reached the diagrammed position.

This situation is not easy to evaluate under conditions of time pressure. It became apparent later that in spite of approximate equality – White has taken a rook, knight and pawn for his queen – and the apparently perilous position of the black king, White is not fully compensated for the loss of his most powerful piece.

After **18 ♗d3 e5! 19 d7 ♗d6 20 ♘e3 ♕xd7 21 f4 ♖d8 22 ♖f1 h6 23 fxe5 ♗c5 24 ♘f5 ♕a4 25 ♖f4 ♔h7** Black managed to evacuate his monarch and initiate decisive action on the queenside. White had spent a lot of time in his search for developing an initiative and, under time presure, let his opponent gain the upper hand.

Salov–Kupreichik
Minsk 1987
(*113*)
Material equality has been disrupted already in this game. How remarkable that such a classical opening as the Queen's Gambit can turn so quickly into a stormy battle: **1 d4 d5 2 c4 dxc4 3 ♘f3 ♘f6 4 e3 e6 5 ♗xc4 c5 6 0-0 a6 7 ♕e2 b5 8 ♗b3 ♗b7 9 ♖d1 ♘bd7**

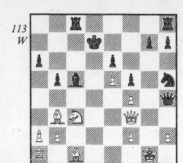

10 e4 cxd4 11 e5 ♗xf3 12 gxf3 ♘h5 13 f4 ♕h4. An interesting novelty, characteristic of the Minsk Grandmaster's creative play. In the game between Timman and Seirawan, Indonesia 1983, after 13 ... g6 14 ♖xd4 ♕b6 15 ♖d1 ♖d8 16 ♘c3 ♗e7 17 f5! White obtained a clear advantage.

14 ♖xd4 ♗c5 15 ♖xd7! The young Leningrad Grandmaster accepts the challenge **15 ... ♔xd7 16 ♕f3 ♖ac8 17 ♘c3 f5!** Having threatened to transpose into an endgame, Black virtually compels his opponent to carry out a little combination with the purpose of forcing a draw by perpetual check. Play continued from the diagram (*113*) as follows: **18 ♗xe6+ ♔xe6 19 ♕d5+ ♔e7 20 ♕b7+** and it seems that the players must agree to a draw immediately. However, true to his uncompromising style, Kupreichik tries, at the cost of a bishop, to avoid perpetual check: **20 ... ♔e6 21 ♕d5+ ♔e7 22 ♕b7+ ♔d8 23 ♕d5+ ♔c7 24 ♕xc5+ ♔b7 25 ♕d5+ ♖c6 26 ♕d7+ ♖c7 27 ♕xf5**.

Again, a position with a dynamic imbalance has been reached. Nevertheless, the game ended in a draw. But spectators in the Minsk Chess Palace were delighted with their local player for the two additional hours to his brilliant performance, played as if for an encore.

Dolmatov–Eingorn
Minsk 1987

From this diagram, a position of a heterogeneous nature was reached after a few moves:

21 ♘xe6 ♗xe3 22 ♖f3 ♕a7 23 cxd5 cxd5 24 ♘xf8 ♘xf8 25 ♕xd5.

White's position looks formidable. However, Black defended stubbornly, managing to retain two minor pieces for a rook. After a ten-hour battle, the game ended in a draw.

Malaniuk–Bareev
Minsk 1987

In this interesting position, in which three minor pieces are on the a-file, White embarked on a series of exchanges: **23 ♗f4 ♕b6 24 bxa3 ♘xc3 25 ♖xb6 ♘xe2 26 ♖b2 ♘xf4 27 ♘xf4 ♗e6 28 ♘h4 ♘c6 29 ♘xf5 ♗xf5 30 ♗xf5 ♘xd4 31 ♘xd5 ♖e8 32 ♗e4 ♖xe5 33 ♖xf7 ♖b8 34 ♘c3 ♘b5** and now instead of **35 ♗g2?** White should have played 35 ♘xb5+ axb5 36 ♗f3, with good winning chances.

Naturally, we could show many more examples of games with heterogeneous imbalance; but the conclusion is obvious.

It appears to us that, arising from the current level of play, there will undoubtedly be a surge in technical knowledge of situations with dynamic imbalance. It appears that this integral branch of the modern middlegame demands a very thorough investigation.